ROBERT LOUIS STEVENSON

LANG SYNE PUBLISHERS LTD.

INTRODUCTION

Publication of this revealing and fascinating biography of Robert Louis Stevenson is a fitting contribution to his centenary. It was compiled shortly after the writer's death in 1894 by Margaret Moyes Black, a friend and close confidante of the family.

Known simply and affectionately to his friends and admirers as R.L.S., the genius who created characters like Long John Silver and Dr Jekyll, was born on November 13, 1850, in Edinburgh. His father and grandfather were lighthouse engineers and his mother the daughter of a minister from Colinton.

In his childhood Robert was a constant invalid but his imagination was fired by stories told by his nurse 'Cummy', Alison Cunningham.

After schooling at Edinburgh Academy young RLS enrolled at the University, studying engineering then law, although he spent more time in the brothels and taverns of the Old Town and Leith Walk.

Travelling in France he met Fanny Osbourne, a married American woman 10 years his senior who he pursued to California, eventually marrying her.

Their early days were spent in poverty but in 1881 RLS completed Treasure Island after a summer holiday in Braemar. It became a great success and was quickly followed by a historical romance, 'The Black Arrow.'

'Kidnapped' and 'The Strange Case of Dr Jekyll and Mr Hyde' were both next, published in 1886.

Two years later came 'The Master of Ballantrae' and throughout this period he produced a string of notable short stories including 'The Bodysnatcher', 'Thrawn Janet', and 'Markheim.'

David Balfour reappeared in the sequel to 'Kidnapped' which RLS called 'Catriona'. 'Weir of Hermiston' might have been his greatest novel but it remained unfinished at the time of the writer's death.

In the summer of 1888 the Stevensons had chartered a yacht to search the Pacific for an island congenial for his tubercular health.

They settled on Samoa where he built his house on the Vailima estate and this is where he died shortly after completing a book of short stories about the South Seas entitled, 'The Beach of Falesa.'

Stevenson's great gifts included a driving narrative energy, strong characterisation, an eye for depicting scenery, and a strange, morbid fascination with the dual nature of good and evil which may have been an intrinsic part of his early personality as well as being typical of many of the figures in his fiction.

In these pages Margaret Moyes Black provides a contemporary, first hand account of Robert Louis Stevenson, a writer of immense talent whose works are still published and read all over the world 100 years after his passing.

LA SOLITUDE
HYÈRES-LES-PALMIERS
VAR Dec 31st 1883

My dear Davie,
at the beginning of the end
of this year, I had many thoughts
of the past, many of yourself, and
many of your mother, who was the
idol of my childhood. I had it in
my mind to write to Uncle David,
but I thought it might be merely
an importunate intrusion, and
decided to write rather to yourself.
The way in which life separates
people is very painful. It is nearly
a year since we had a New Year's
walk; but I have not forgotten the
past, and your mother I shall never
forget. I am profoundly a Stevenson
in the matter of not giving presents

PHOTOGRAPH OF AN UNPUBLISHED LETTER OF R. L. S.'s.

Once only that I can remember did I, of my own motion, give a present; and that was before '57, when I "asked leave" to give a present to Aunt Elizabeth. I do not suppose that a greater testimony could be given to her extraordinary charm and kindness. I never saw anybody like her: a look from Aunt Elizabeth was like sunshine.

Please excuse this very blundering scrawl; understand what is unsaid; and accept, for yourself and all in the family, my most sincere good wishes

Your affectionate cousin
Robert Louis Stevenson

Published by Lang Syne Publishers Ltd.
Clydeway Centre, 45 Finnieston Street, Glasgow
and printed by Scotprint, Musselburgh.
© LANG SYNE PUBLISHERS LTD. 1994.
ISBN 185217 0107
This is a facsimile of the biography first published in 1898
in the Famous Scots Series.
The covers feature favourite photographs of the author.

CONTENTS

8 CONTENTS

CHAPTER VIII

CHAPTER IX

CHAPTER X

CHAPTER XI

CHAPTER XII

CHAPTER XIII

ROBERT LOUIS STEVENSON

CHAPTER I

HEREDITY AND ANTECEDENTS

'These are thy works, O father, these thy crown,
Whether on high the air be pure they shine
Along the yellowing sunset, and all night
Among the unnumbered stars of God they shine.
Or whether fogs arise, and far and wide
The low sea-level drown—each finds a tongue,
And all night long the tolling bell resounds.
So shine so toll till night be overpast,
Till the stars vanish, till the sun return,
And in the haven rides the fleet at last.'
—R. L. STEVENSON.

IN no country in the world is heredity more respected than in Scotland, and her hard-working sons freely acknowledge the debt they owe, for the successes of to-day, to the brave struggle with sterner conditions of life their ancestors waged from generation to generation. We of the present are 'the heirs of all the ages'; but we are also in no small degree the clay from the potter's hands, moulded and kneaded by the natures, physical and mental, of those who have gone before us, and whose lives and circumstances have made us what we are.

Robert Lewis Balfour Stevenson—for so the writer

whom the world knows as Robert Louis Stevenson, was baptised—valued greatly this doctrine of heredity, and always bore enthusiastic testimony to the influence his ancestry and antecedents had exercised in moulding his temperament and character. He was proud of that ancestry, with no foolish pride, but rather with that appreciation of all that was noble and worthy in his fore-fathers, which made him desire to be, in his own widely differing life-work, as good a man as they.

> . . . 'And I—can I be base?'—he says;
> 'I must arise, O father, and to port
> Some lost complaining seaman pilot home.'

He had reason to think highly of the honourable name which he received from his father's family. Britain and the whole world has much for which to thank the Steven-sons; not only all along our rough north coasts, but in every part of the world where the mariner rejoices to see their beacon's blaze have the firm, who are consulting engineers to the Indian, the New Zealand, and the Japanese Lighthouse Boards, lit those lights of which Rudyard Kipling in his 'Songs of the English,' sings—

> 'Our brows are bound with spindrift, and the weed is on our knees;
> Our loins are battered 'neath us by the swinging, smoking seas;
> From reef and rock and skerry, over headland, ness, and voe,
> The coastguard lights of England watch the ships of England go.'

Wild and wind-swept are the isles and headlands of the northern half of the sister kingdoms, but from their dreariest points the lights that have been kindled by Robert Stevenson, the hero of Bell Rock fame, and his descendants flash and flame across the sea, and make the name of Stevenson a word of blessing to the storm-tossed sailor.

The author was third in descent from that Robert Stevenson, who, by skill and heroism, planted the lighthouse on the wave-swept Bell Rock—only uncovered for the possibility of work for a short time at low tides—and made safety on the North Sea, where before there had been death and danger, from the cruel cliffs that guard that iron coast.

What child has not thrilled and shivered over the ballad of 'Ralph the Rover,' who, hoping doubtless that the wrecked ships might fall into his own piratical hands, cut the bell which the good monks of Aberbrothock had placed on the fatal rock, and who, by merited justice, was for lack of the bell himself, on his return voyage, lost on that very spot! What boy has not loved the story of one of the greatest engineering feats that patience and skill has ever accomplished!

If other young folk so loved it what a depth of interest must not that noble story have had for the grandson of the hero, whose childish soul was full of chivalry and romance, and whose boyish eyes saw visions of the future and pictures of the past as no ordinary child could see them, for his was the gift of genius, and even the commonplace things of life were glorified to him.

Alan Stevenson, who was the father of Robert, died of fever when in the island of St Christopher on a visit to his brother, who managed the foreign business of the Glasgow West India house with which they were connected. The brother unfortunately dying of the same fever, business matters were somewhat complicated, and

Alan's widow and little boy had to endure straitened circumstances. The mother strained every nerve to have
her boy, whom she intended for the ministry, well educated, and the lad profited by her self-denial. Her second
marriage, however, very fortunately changed her plans
for Robert, for her second husband, Mr Smith, had a
mechanical bent which led him to make many researches
on the subject of lighting and lighthouses, and finding
that his stepson shared his tastes, he encouraged him in
his engineering and mechanical studies.

The satisfactory results of Mr Smith's researches caused
the first Board of Northern Lights to make him their
engineer, and he designed Kinnaird Head, the first
light they exhibited, and illuminated it in 1787. He
was succeeded as engineer to the Board by his stepson, of Bell Rock fame, and his grandson, Mr David
Alan Stevenson, who now holds the post, is the sixth in
the family who has done so.   Young Stevenson not only
became his stepfather's partner but married his eldest
daughter, and with her founded a home that was evidently
a happy one, for the great engineer was a most unselfish
character, and made an excellent husband and father.
He was a notable volunteer in the days when a French
invasion was greatly feared, and all his life he took a keen
interest in the volunteering movement.

Like his son Thomas, Mr Robert Stevenson was a man
of much intellect and humour, though of a grave and
serious character.   He was also a keen Conservative and
a loving member of the Established Church of Scotland.
He was warmly beloved and his society was greatly sought
after by his friends ; a voyage of inspection with him on

his tours round the coast was much appreciated. On one occasion—in 1814—Sir Walter Scott made one of the party which accompanied him. Mr Robert Stevenson died in July 1850, a few months before the birth of his grandson, Robert Louis.

That this grandson held in high esteem the deeds and sterling qualities of his grandfather is amply proved by his Samoan Letters to Mr Sidney Colvin, published in 1895. In many of them he speaks of the history of his family, which he intended to write, and into which he evidently felt that he could put his best work. Alas! like so much that the brave spirit and the busy brain planned, it was not to be, and the writer passed to his rest without leaving behind him a full record of the workers who had made his name famous.*

Mr Alan, Mr David, and Mr Thomas Stevenson worthily handed on the traditions of their father, and in its second generation the lustre of the great engineering family shone undimmed; while now the sons of David Stevenson maintain the reputation of their forefathers, and the Stevenson name is still one to conjure with wherever their saving lights shine out across the sea.

Mr Thomas Stevenson served for a short time under his brother Alan in building the famous lighthouse of 'Skerryvore.' In 1846 he was taken into partnership by his brother David—the firm being known as D. & T. Stevenson—and with him he built 'The Chickens,' 'Dhu Heartach,' and many 'shore lights' and harbours. He was a not-

* The portion of this family history—*Family of Engineers*—which Mr Stevenson had completed, at the time of his death, is to be found in 'The Edinburgh Edition' of his works.

able engineer, widely known and greatly honoured at home and abroad, besides being a very typical Scotsman.

When one thinks of his grand rugged face, and re-members how the stern eyes used to light up with humour and soften with tenderness, as their glance fell on his wife and his son, one realises what a very perfect picture of such a character in its outward sternness and its inward gentleness, lies in those lines of Mr William Watson's, in which he speaks of

'The fierceness that from tenderness is never far.'

Mr Stevenson's broad shoulders, his massive head, his powerful face, reminded one of that enduring grey Scotch stone from which he and his ancestors raised round all our coasts, their lighthouses and harbours.

Strong, grey, silent, these solid blocks resist winds and waves, and so one felt would that powerful reti-cent nature stand steadfast in life's battle, a tower of strength to those who trusted him.   Like his firm's 'Beacon Lights,' on cliff and headland brilliant gleams of humour bright gems of genius flashed out now and then from the silence.   One felt too that safe as the ships in his splendid harbours, would rest family and friends in the strong yet loving heart that could hold secure all that it valued through the tests and changes of time and the conflicts of varying thoughts and oppos-ing opinions.   A man of strong prejudices, a man too of varying moods, Mr Stevenson knew what it was at times to endure hours of depression, to suffer from an almost morbidly religious conscience, but he always kept a courageous hold on life and found the best cure for a shadowed soul lay in constant and varied work.

The charming dedication of *Familiar Studies of Men and Books* is a delightful tribute from the gifted son to the strength and nobility of his father's character.

Highly favoured in his paternal heredity Mr R. L. Stevenson was no less fortunate in his mother and his mother's family.

If strength and force of intellect characterised Mr Thomas Stevenson, his wife, Margaret Balfour, had no less powerful an individuality; in beauty of person, in grace of manner, in the brilliance of a quick and flashing feminine intelligence — that was deep as well as bright — she was a fitting helpmate for her husband, and the very mother to sympathise with and encourage a son whose genius showed itself in quaint sayings, in dainty ways, and in chivalrous thoughts almost from his infancy.

Mrs Stevenson was the youngest daughter of the Rev. Dr Lewis Balfour, from 1823 to 1860 minister of Colinton, and of Henrietta Scott Smith, daughter of the minister of Galston. There had been thirteen children in the manse of Colinton, and father and mother had made of the picturesque old house a home in truth as well as in name. Many of these children survived long enough, two of them indeed are still living, to carry the sacred traditions of that happy home out into a world where they made honourable positions for themselves.

After the death of the mother her place was taken by her daughter Jane, that aunt of whom Robert Louis

Stevenson wrote so sweetly in his *Child's Garden of Verses*—

> 'Chief of our Aunts not only I
> But all your other nurslings cry,
> What did the other children do?
> And what were childhood wanting you?'

To other 'motherless bairns,' as well as to her own brothers and sisters, nephews and nieces, that most motherly heart and gentle and beautiful soul has been a comfort and a refuge on the thorny highway of life, and many whose love she has earned by the tenderness of her sympathy still call Miss Balfour blessed.

She was a true helper to her father in the motherless home and in his parish work, and in spite of much bad health filled the mother's place in the house and won for herself the undying affection and regard not only of her own family but of her father's parishioners and friends.

A testimony to the high esteem in which her father's memory and hers, and indeed that of all the Balfour family, is still held in Colinton, was given to me a few years ago by the old beadle there.   Fond as he was of Dr Lockhart, to speak to him of the Balfours, whom he remembered in his younger days, at once won his attention and regard. On my saying to him it was for their sakes I wished to see the inside of the church he queried with a brightening face :

'Ye'll no be ane o' them, will ye?'

'No' was the reply, 'but they have been so long known and loved they seem like my " ain folk " to me.'

'Aweel come awa' an' see the kirk.   Will ye mind o' him?'

Alas ! no ; for the minister of Colinton had died seven years before my friendship with the Balfours began.

' Eh ! ' was all the old man said, but that and the shake of his head eloquently expressed what a loss that was for me !

' But ye'll ken *her* ? ' meaning Miss Balfour, he queried again, and as I said I did and well, the face brightened with a great brightness.

So, having found a friend in common, together we went over the church and the manse grounds, but, as Dr Lockhart was away from home, I resisted his persuasion to ask leave to go through the house and contented myself with a pleasant talk with him of Dr John Balfour, who had fought the mutineers in India and the cholera at Davidson's Mains, Slateford, and Leven ; of Dr George, who is still fighting the ills that flesh is heir to, in Edinburgh ; of the sons and daughters of the manse who had gone to their rest ; of Mrs Stevenson, then in Samoa with her son, and whose charm of personality made her dear to the old man, and lastly of ' the clivir lad,' her son, who had spent such happy days in the old manse garden.

Of all the children in that large family Maggie, the youngest, was perhaps especially her sister's charge ; and one knows, from that elder sister's description, how sweet, and good, and bright the little girl was, and how charming was the face, and how loving the heart of the mother of Robert Louis Stevenson when she too was a child at play in the manse garden. The mother's beauty and that dainty refinement of face and voice which she bequeathed

to her son came to her in a long and honourable descent
from a family that had for centuries been noted for the
beauty and the sincere goodness of its women, for the
godliness and the manliness of its men.

The Rev. Dr Lewis Balfour of Colinton was the third
son of Mr Balfour, the Laird of Pilrig. The quaint old
house of Pilrig stands a little back from Leith Walk, the
date on it is 1638; and the text inscribed on its door-
stone, 'For we know, that if our earthly house of this
tabernacle were dissolved we have a building of God, an
house not made with hands eternal in the heavens,' is a
fitting motto for a race whose first prominent ancestor
was that James Balfour of Reformation times, who not
only was a cousin of Melville the Reformer, but who
married one of the Melville family. This double tie to
those so entwined with the very life of that great period
in Scotland's history brought Mr James Balfour into very
close communion with such men as Erskine of Dun, the
Rev. John Durie, and many others of the Reforming
ministers and gentlemen, with whom a member of the
Pilrig family, the late James Balfour-Melville, Esq., W.S.,
in his interesting pamphlet dealing with his family says,
that his ancestor had much godly conversation and
communing.

The early promise of the race was not belied in its
later descendants, and the Balfours were noted for their
zeal in religion, and in their country's affairs, as well as
for an honourable and prudent application to the business of life on their own account. Andrew Balfour, the
minister of Kirknewton, signed the protestation for the
Kirk in 1617, and was imprisoned for it. His son

James was called to the Scotch Bar, and was a Clerk of Session in Cromwell's time. A son of his was a Governor of the Darien Company, and his son, in turn, purchased the estate of Pilrig where his descendants kept up the godly and honourable traditions of the house, and dispensed a pleasant and a kindly hospitality to their friends in Edinburgh, from whom, at that time, their pretty old home was somewhat distant in the country!

With such an ancestry on both sides one can easily understand the bent of Robert Louis Stevenson's mind towards old things, the curious traditions of Scotch family history and the lone wild moorlands,

> ' Where about the graves of the martyrs
> The whaups are calling,'

one can comprehend, too, the attraction for him of the power and the mystery of the sea. All these things came to him as a natural inheritance from those who had gone before, and in the characters who people his books, in *Kidnapped*, in *Catriona*, in *Weir of Hermiston*, we see live again, the folk of that older Edinburgh, whom those by-gone Balfours knew.

In the fresh salt breeze that, as it were, blows keen from the sea in *Treasure Island*, in *The Merry Men*, and about the sad house of Durrisdeer in *The Master of Ballantrae*, we recognise the magic wooing of the mighty ocean that made of the Stevensons builders of lighthouses and harbours, and masters of the rough, wild coasts where the waves beat and the spray dashes, and the sea draws all who love it to ride upon its breast in ships.

From the union of two families who have been so long

and so honourably known in their different ways, there came much happiness, and one feels somewhat sorry that when Louis Stevenson signed his name to the books by which he is so lovingly remembered, he did not write it in full and spell 'Lewis' in the old-time fashion that was good enough for our Scotch ancestors in the days when many a 'Lewis' drew sword for Gustavus Adolphus, or served as a gentleman volunteer in the wars of France or the Netherlands, and when 'O, send Lewie Gordon hame' rang full of pathos to the Scotch ears, to which the old spelling was familiar. Mr Stevenson's Balfour relatives naturally regret the alteration of the older spelling and the omission of his mother's family name from his signature. With regard to the latter, he himself assured his mother that having merely dropped out the Balfour to shorten a very long name, he greatly regretted having done so, after it was too late, and he had won his literary fame as 'Robert Louis Stevenson,' and much wished that he had invariably written his name as R. L. Balfour Stevenson. The spelling of Lewis he altered when he was about eighteen, in deference to a wish of his father's, as at one time the elder Mr Stevenson had a prejudice against the name of Lewis, so his son thereafter signed himself Louis. That he may have himself also preferred it is very possible ; he was fond of all things French, and he may have liked the link to that far off ancestor, the French barber-surgeon who landed at St Andrews to be one of the suite of Cardinal Beaton ! In spite of the belief on the part of Robert Louis, who had a fancy to the contrary, the name in the Balfour family was *invariably* spelt Lewis. His grandfather was christened

Lewis, and so the entry of his name remains to this day in the old family Bible at Pilrig ; so also it is spelt in that, already mentioned, most interesting pamphlet for private circulation, written by the late James Balfour-Melville, Esq., who gives the name of his uncle, the minister of Colinton, as Lewis Balfour, and so the old clergyman signed himself all his life.

CHAPTER II

CHILDHOOD

. . . 'With love divine
My mother's fingers folded mine.'
—FROM VERSES IN AN AMERICAN PAPER.

' We built a ship upon the stairs,
All made of the back bedroom chairs ;
And filled it full of sofa pillows,
To go a-sailing on the billows.'
—R. L. STEVENSON.

MR AND MRS THOMAS STEVENSON, who were married in
1848, made their first home at 8 Howard Place, and
there, on 13th November 1850, Robert Lewis Balfour
Stevenson was born. In 1853 they moved to a house
in Inverleith Terrace, and in 1857, when Louis was
about seven years old, they took possession of 17 Heriot
Row, the house so long and so intimately associated with
them in the minds of their many friends.

The little Louis was from his earliest babyhood a very
delicate child, and only the most constant and tender
care of his devoted mother and nurse enabled him to
survive those first years which must have been so full
of anxiety to his parents. In *The Child's Garden of
Verses* there are some lines called ' The Land of Counterpane,' the picture heading of which is a tiny child propped
up against his bed pillows, and with all his toys scattered

on the coverlet.   Beneath it are four verses that give a
wonderfully graphic description of the life the little boy
too often led.

In the last verse he was a giant who saw before him all
'the pleasant land of counterpane,' and in the very word
'pleasant' the temperament of the child shows itself.
How many children would have found anything 'pleasant'
in the enforced days of lie-a-bed quietness, and would
have made no murmurs over the hard fate which forbade
to them the active joys of other boys and girls ?

But this small lad had a sweet temper and an unselfish,
contented disposition, and so he bore the burden of his
bad health as bravely in those days as he did in after
years, and made for himself plays and pleasures with his
nimble brain while his weary body was often tired and
restless in that bed whereof he had so much. His mother
used to describe, with the same graphic touch that gives
life to all her son wrote, the bright games the little fellow
invented for himself when he was well enough to be
up and about, and tell how, in a corner of the room, he
made for himself a wonder-world all his own, in which
heroes and heroines of romance loved and fought and
walked and talked at the bidding of the wizard in frock
and pinafore.

It was not all indoor life happily, and if there were
many bad days there were some good and glad ones also,
when he was well and allowed to be out and at play in the
world of outdoor life he always loved so dearly.

Two quaint pictures of the child as he was in those
days have been supplied by his aunt, Miss Balfour. One
of them is from a note-book of his mother's, in which she

had jotted down a few things that had been said or written of him. The first interesting description is that given by a very dear old friend of the family, and is an exceedingly early one, for it was written in October 1853, when Louis was barely three, and the family had just settled in Inverleith Terrace.

'One day,' she says, 'I called and missed you, and found Cummie' (the valued nurse) 'and Louis just starting for town, so we walked up together by Canonmills, keeping the middle of the road all the way.'

Louis, she continues, was dressed in a navy blue pelisse trimmed with fur, a beaver hat, a fur ruff, and white gloves. A very quaint little figure he must have been with the thin delicate face and the wonderfully bright eyes, so luminous and far-seeing even then!

The tiny mite repeated hymns all the way, 'emphasising so prettily,' the friend goes on to say, 'with the dear little baby hands. All of a sudden, when near St Mary's Church he stood still, and looking in my face, said:

' " But by-the-bye did I ever give you my likeness ? "

' " No," was the reply, " have you got your likeness ? "

' " Oh ! yes, I will give it you ; I will send it by the *real* post to-morrow." '

'It seemed,' the lady adds, 'as if the wonderful little mind had been considering what other kind thing he could do besides repeating the hymns.'

The whole incident is an excellent example of his sweetness of disposition, and his innate thoughtfulness for others. It is pleasant to know that the pretty promise was fulfilled, Mrs Stevenson herself acting 'postman,' and taking the likeness to her friend next day.

The second picture is from the memory of Miss Balfour herself. She too describes the blue pelisse trimmed with grey astrakhan, which he wore in the winter of 1853 and '54. In the spring of 1854 she went to the Stevensons' house to tell her sister that their father had been given the degree of Doctor of Divinity. The small Louis, on hearing his grandfather spoken of as 'Doctor,' immediately said:

'Now that grandpapa is a doctor, surely you'll have him instead of Dr Hunter?'

A wonderfully quick thought and old-fashioned remark from a child not four years old, but a suggestively sad one too ; he already knew so well the necessity of a doctor to help human bodies, although he could not yet comprehend the use of one for the 'cure' of human souls!

When he heard that his aunt was going to see a relative in Saxe Coburg Place, he begged to be allowed to go with her, and, the permission granted, started off in great pride on his very first expedition without his nurse, that faithful friend of the Stevenson family having promised to follow later to take him home. The aunt at least had cause to remember that walk! He had started gloveless, and would not go back for his gloves, but popped his cold hands under the cape of his pelisse, and even then, unconventional as to clothing, said cheerfully:

'That will keep them from John Frost.'

So the pair set out on what proved a chilly and prolonged excursion ; for, in spite of all remonstrances, the child calmly sat down on every doorstep and rested till he felt inclined to go on again, to the no small dismay of his aunt, who knew how serious a thing the taking of a cold was to the placid little personage smiling at her from the steps.

During the Crimean war, while he was still a very tiny mite, he, entirely of his own accord, always prayed for the soldiers. When asked by his mother if he would like to be a soldier, his answer was—

'I would neither like to kill nor to be killed,'—a very sensible reason to have been thought out by so young a child.

His aunt says of him—'I never knew so sweet a child.'

And his mother always said of him that his sweetness and patience were beautiful. On one subject only mother and child sometimes differed. Louis wished her to agree with him that grandpapa's home was the nicest in the world, but the mother maintained their own home was best.

Until his grandfather died in 1860, when he was ten years old, the manse at Colinton was the little boy's favourite abiding place. Here 'Auntie' lived, and near here, too, was the home of the 'sister-cousin,' and her brother who grew up with him, and who, of all the much loved cousins of that large connection, were nearest and dearest in his child-life, and to whom he sings—

> ' If two may read aright
> These rhymes of old delight,
> And house and garden play
> You two, my cousins, and you only may.

> ' You in a garden green,
> With me were king and queen,
> Were soldier, hunter, tar,
> And all the thousand things that children are.'

With these two cousins the favourite game was the fleeing from, conquering, and finally slaying a huge giant called Bunker, invented by Louis, who, the trio believed, haunted the manse garden, and required continual killing. One time, on the Bonaly Road, they were shipwrecked hungry sailors, who ate so many buttercups that the little boys were poisoned and became very ill, and the little girl only escaped because she found the flowers too bitter to eat! In the ' Redford burn of happy memories ' they sailed ships richly laden with whin pods for vanilla, and yellow lichen for gold.   They always hoped to see ghosts, or corpse candles, and were much disappointed they never saw anything more terrible, in the gruesome place where the sexton kept his tools, than a swaying branch of ivy.

Of the tall, pale, venerable grandfather, with his snowy hair, Louis stood a good deal in awe ; and he tells us in his charming paper, ' The Manse,' in *Memories and Portraits*, that he had not much in common with the old man although he felt honoured by his connection with a person reverend enough to enter the pulpit and preach the sermon every Sunday. So many Balfours were scattered over the world, in India and the Colonies, that the old rooms at the manse were full of eastern curiosities and nick-nacks from distant lands dear to the hearts of little folks. And, while the garden was a bower of delight, the house was a veritable treasure trove to the grandchildren from far and near who played in it.

To Robert Louis Stevenson, with his mind full of romance, it must have been a paradise indeed, and one that he admirably pictures in the verses addressed to an

Anglo-Indian cousin who, as a married woman, has returned to the India of her birth.

It is worth mentioning—as a note by the way which illustrates that abiding boyishness in Mr Stevenson, so well known to all who knew him—that four particularly hideous Indian idols stood guard at the hall door of 'The Turret,' the house of his uncle, John Balfour, at Leven. Two of them were life-size with their hands discreetly folded in prayer, two of them were smaller and made in a kneeling posture, and, as something rattled if you shook them, it was our juvenile belief that treasure was concealed inside their bodies. This idea Mr R. L. Stevenson eagerly fostered in the slightly younger generation, and, with the love of harmless mischief natural to him, implored us to 'rattle them *soundly* when we were about it !'

In the manse garden at Colinton there was a mysterious and delightful gap that gave egress to the Water of Leith, and to pass through this and stray, out of safe and guarded precincts, into a wide and wet world beyond was a keen pleasure to the little boy whose gipsy instincts were already loudly calling to him to take 'the road' his wandering soul so dearly loved.

'Keepsake Mill' is a charming tribute to the joys of those illicit escapes and to the memories of the cousin playfellows now scattered in far lands, or for ever at rest from life's labour, who played in the garden where the delicate bright-eyed lad was the inventor and leader in their games.

One sweet fancy of the imaginative child, who all his life had a fine mental and physical courage in spite of his delicacy, is still recalled by his ' sister-cousin '; the grave-

yard wall was at one place high above the garden it
partially enclosed, and the little boy, afflicted with no
superstitious terrors, had an idea that the souls of the
dead people at rest in 'God's acre,' peeped out at him
from the chinks of the wall.   And one feels sure that
here as all through his life, shadowed by so much of
suffering, he held fast, after a fashion of his own, the
belief that goes deeper than his playful rendering of it in
The Unseen Playmate seems at first to infer :

> ' Whene'er you're happy and cannot tell why,
> The Friend of the children is sure to be by.'

A faith that was taught him by an earnest father and by
the loving voice of a mother who held it fast through
her own happy childhood and the joys and sorrows that
as wife and mother came to her in later years.

After the death of the Rev. Dr Balfour, in April 1860,
the manse ceased to be the second home of Louis
Stevenson, and in the November of that year his aunt,
Miss Balfour, and the nephews and nieces who stayed
with her moved to a house in Howard Place.

In 1858 he went to school, and from 1860 to 1861
he and his cousin, Lewis Charles Balfour, were together
at Mr Henderson's preparatory school in India Street
from which both went to the Academy in 1861.   Of
Lewis Stevenson,— who in later life was always called
Louis or Lou by his family and friends,—Mr Henderson
reports : ' Robert's reading is not loud, but impressive.'

In July he was in bed with scarlet fever on his ex-
amination day, which was a great disappointment to him.
He had a first prize for reading that year ; but his zeal

over school and lessons was very short-lived, and he never hungered for scholastic honours.

As a child he did not learn quickly, and he was in his eighth year before he could read fluently for himself. Nevertheless his especial bent showed itself early, and when in his sixth year he dictated a *History of Moses*, which he illustrated, giving the men pipes in their mouths. This, and an account of *Travels in Perth*, composed in his ninth year, are still in existence. The *History of Moses* was written because an uncle had offered a prize to his own children for the best paper on the subject, and the little Louis was so disappointed at not being asked to compete that he was finally included among the competitors, and did a paper which though not best was still good and which was given a prize. He had begun to print it for himself, with much toil, but his mother offered to write it out from his dictation. Another composition of this time was a fierce story of shipwreck and fighting with savages.

In 1863 he was sent for a few months to a boarding school kept by a Mr Wyatt at Spring Grove, near London. Life at a boarding school was misery to a lad so fond of wandering at his own sweet will as the small Louis, and he was full of distress at the prospect of leaving home. In *Random Memories* he gives his ideas as to going to school, and expresses his belief that it is not so much the first night or day at school that is so terrible to a courageous child, as the dismay at the thought of leaving home with its familiar life and surroundings, and the painful suspense for some days before the plunge into the new world of school is taken. It was, he says, this miserable feeling of suspense that made him share his sorrows with a desolate, but amiable cat in the Easter Road, which mingled its woes with his and as it purred against him consoled him.

His tender-hearted parents were so touched by his evident affliction, and especially by the little story of the cat, that his father took him a trip round the coast of Fife in *The Pharos* and he thus made an early and delightful acquaintance with some of the lights and harbours which his father had gone to inspect.

The cousin Lewis Charles Balfour, who had been his schoolfellow in Edinburgh, and two of his younger brothers, were day pupils at the Spring Grove School, and his aunt, Miss Balfour, was living near. Robert Lewis was not very much attached to boarding-school life, except when it took the form of sardine suppers, 'under the rose'; and regular work was never greatly to his liking. His father, who had been alone in Edinburgh, went for him in December and took him to join his mother, who was wintering at Mentone. Both were anxious to arrive by Christmas Day, and travelled so quickly that father and son became ill, the boy so seriously that Dr Henry Bennett had to prescribe some very bracing treatment.

Of the home where so much consideration was shown to a child's health and feelings, no better description can be given than the graphic one of a little Stevenson cousin who had gone with his parents to stay there, and who thus spoke of it : 'A child who never cries, a nurse who is never cross, and late dinners.'

Can one imagine a dignified, childish paradise that could go much further ! Nor were the joys of books

awanting to the happy small boy who describes himself
as in early days being carried off by his nurse

> 'To bed with backward looks,
> At my dear world of story books.'

As soon as he had learned to read he was an eager
and an omnivorous reader, and could, from his eighth
year, pass happy hours with a book, any book so long
as it did not mean lessons.

He was before very long a book-buyer as well as a
book-lover, and he has for ever immortalised, in the
charming pages of *A Penny Plain and Twopence
Coloured*, that old bookshop (late J. L. Smith) at the
corner of Leith Walk, where eager boys without coppers
were but coldly received, but whence the fortunate
capitalist could emerge, after having spent his Saturday
pocket-money, the proud possessor of plays positively
bristling with pirates and highwaymen. With these
treasures he fled home in the gathering dusk, while
'Leerie-Light-the-Lamps' was kindling his cheery beacons
along the streets, and, with pleasant terrors, devoured the
weird productions, finally adding to their weirdness by
the garish contents of a child's paint-box.

CHAPTER III

BOYHOOD AND COLLEGE DAYS

'A boy's will is the wind's will,
And the thoughts of youth are long, long thoughts.'
—LONGFELLOW.

. . . 'Strange enchantments from the past
And memories of the friends of old,
And strong tradition binding fast
The "flying terms" with bands of gold.'
—ANDREW LANG.

THE years 1861 and 1862 found Louis, with his childhood left behind him, a boy among other boys who sat on the forms and who played in the yards of the Academy, at which, during the greater part of the present century, many of the sons of Edinburgh men, and indeed of Scotsmen everywhere at home and abroad, have received their education.

From 1864 to 1867 he was principally at a Mr Thompson's school in Frederick Street, and he studied from time to time with private tutors at the different places to which his parents went for the benefit of their own health or his. These rather uncommon educational experiences were of far more value to him in after life than a steady attendance at any one school, as they made him an excellent linguist and gave him, from very youth-

ful years, a wide knowledge of foreign life and foreign
manners.   In 1862 the Stevenson family visited Holland
and Germany, in 1863 they were in Italy, in 1864 in
the Riviera, and at Torquay for some months during
the winter of 1865 and 1866 ; but after 1867 the family
life became more settled and was chiefly passed between
Edinburgh and Swanston.

In those days Louis was a lean, slim lad, inclined to
be tall, and with soft, somewhat lank, brown hair and
brown eyes of a shade that seemed to deepen and change
with every passing impression of his quick working brain.
His features were rather long, the upper part of his
narrow face was delicately formed like his mother's,
but the lips were full, and a more virile strength in chin
and jaw faintly reminded one of his father's powerful
physiognomy.

He had opinions of his own in regard to education,
and they by no means led him to consider a strict
attendance at school or a close application to lessons as
necessary for his future life-work.   He read, it is true,
voraciously, but it was hardly on the lines of the sternly
respectable classical curriculum which his tutors or the
Academy offered him.   He was an historical student
after a fashion of his own, dipping deep into such books
of bygone romance as Sir Walter Scott had conned
and loved.   His geography at that time took a purely
practical and somewhat limited form, and resolved itself
into locating correctly the places and abodes sacred to
the characters in his favourite books.

In the delightful dedication of *Catriona*, — to Mr
Charles Baxter, W.S., Edinburgh, who was his life-long

friend—he describes those pilgrimages charmingly, and
one can, in imagination, see the eager lads wandering in
search of famous 'streets and numbered houses,' made
historic for them by some such magic pen as that which
has for ever made sacred the *Old Tolbooth* or the *Heart
of Midlothian*, from the coblestones of which, in the
pavement of St Giles and near the Parliament House,
one reverently steps aside lest careless feet should touch
that memento of the past.   One can picture too as he
himself does, the romantic boys of to-day following the
wanderings of David Balfour by Broughton and Silver-
mills, the Water of Leith, the Hawes Inn at Queensferry,
and the windswept shores of the Forth.   But one can
still more clearly see that slim, brown-eyed youth—
a-quiver with the eagerness that was so conspicuous a
characteristic of his,—as in these very places he remembered bygone tales and even then formed plans
for, and saw visions of, his own stories yet to be.

One can think of him with his eyes shining, and his
face luminous, as he held forth to some choice friend, of
sympathetic soul, on all these things of which his heart
and brain were so full.   One knows that when his walks
were solitary his time was already put to a good account,
and that the note-books which even then he carried in his
pocket were in constant requisition.

The boy, from the very first, felt a strong leading to the
profession of letters, which he ultimately followed ; and he
describes himself as from very early boyhood having been
given to make notes for possible romances, and to choose
words of peculiar fitness for the purpose he had in hand,
as well as to weave tales of thrilling adventure.

Style was from the first a passion with him ; and the
lad had already begun in these juvenile note-books that
careful choice of words and language which was at the
very outset of his literary career to make so competent a
critic as Mr Hamerton call him one of the greatest living
masters of English prose.   That he became something of
a master in verse also those few thin volumes of deep
thoughts, in a setting of fitly chosen words and rhymes,
which he has published, amply prove.

To return, however, to the boy who went to the
Academy, or rather who did *not* go to the Academy, for
he had a faculty for playing truant which must have been
extraordinarily provoking to parents and masters.   No
sooner was he out of the door in the morning than he
could truly say—

> ‘ I heard the winds, with unseen feet,
> Pass up the long and weary street,
>
> ‘ They say “ We come from hill and glen
> To touch the brows of toiling men.”
>
> ‘ That each may know and feel we bring
> The faint first breathings of the spring.’

And the voice of the spring thus calling him as soon as
it was heard, was obeyed ; and, careless of the frowns that
were bound to greet his return, he was off to wander on
his beloved Braids and Pentlands, to lie long days among
the whin and the broom, or to slip away to watch the
busy shipping on the Forth, and to think deep thoughts
beside the wave-washed shore of that sea which ever drew
him like the voice of a familiar friend.

To that intense love of Nature, and of Nature’s solitude, his readers owe much, and we to-day may all say with the writer who gave such an interesting description of Swanston in *Good Words* in the spring of 1895, that those truant hours of his educated him for his future work far better than a careful attendance at school and college could have done. The same writer says that it was this open air life that he loved so dearly which gave to Stevenson's books their large leisure, and to his style its dignity. There is much truth in the remark ; but as far as the style is concerned it is the product of time and thought, and it was most carefully and diligently formed by labour so earnest and painstaking, that few authors can even conceive of it.

In *Memories and Portraits* Mr Stevenson gives a delightful account of boyish days at a seaside resort, that is evidently North Berwick, and lovingly describes adventures with bull's-eye lanterns ; adventures which seem to be intimately associated with the young folk of his connection, and which repeated themselves a few years later on the other side of the Forth, where boys and girls recalled the doings of Robert Louis and his friends with bull's-eye lanterns and gunpowder, in that cheerful form known to Louis Stevenson as a ' peeoy,' and considered it a point of honour to do likewise, no matter how indignant such mischief made the authorities. As for him, he was always the inventor and prime mover in every mischievous escapade the heart of youth could glory in.

The wind-swept coast about North Berwick had a strong fascination for him, and in several of his books we feel the salt breeze blowing in from the sea, across the bents, and hear the sea birds crying on the lonely shore. The autumn

holidays were a great joy to him, and another epoch-making
event must have been the taking of Swanston Cottage,
in May 1867, to be the summer home of the Stevensons.

The boy took intense pleasure in his rambles about the
hills, in his dreamy rests on 'Kirk Yetton' * and 'Aller-
muir,' and in his wanderings with John Todd, the shepherd,
after that worthy had ceased, as he comically puts it, to
hunt him off as a dangerous sheep-scarer, and so to play
'Claverhouse to his Covenanter'! The two soon became
great friends, and many a bit of strange philosophy, many
a wild tale of bygone droving days the lad heard from
the old man.   Another great friend of early Swanston
years was Robert Young, the gardener, whose austere
and Puritan views of life were solemnly shared with his
young master.

Existence at Swanston was even more provocative of
truant-playing than it had been in Edinburgh, and Louis,
in his later school days and his early sessions at the
University, was more than ever conspicuous by his absence
from classes, more lovingly wedded to long hours among
the hills, long rambles about the 'Old Town,' the Figgate
Whins, the port of Leith, and the rapidly changing localities round Leith Walk, somewhat back from which, Pilrig,
the ancient home of his ancestors, still stands gravely
retired from the work-a-day world.

In the year 1867 he went with his father to the 'Dhu
Heartach' Lighthouse, and so began to develop that
passion for the Western Isles and the Western seas
which future voyages in *The Pharos* were to bring to

* Cairketton is the form used in the Ordnance Survey.

the state of fervour and perfection which gave birth of *The Merrymen*, and to those descriptions of the wild and lovely scenery of Appin and the West Highlands, in which David Balfour and Alan Breck wander through the pages of *Kidnapped*.

It was his father's intention that he should follow the family profession of engineering, and with this in view he went to the Edinburgh University in the autumn of 1868. The professors in those days included Professors Kelland, Tait, Crum-Brown, Fleeming-Jenkin, Blackie, Masson, and many others whose names are still remembered as 'a sweet-smelling savour' in that Edinburgh which they and the truant student, who honoured his class attendance 'more in the breach than the observance,' loved so well.

It was a stirring time at the University, and the students who warred manfully against the innovation of Dr Sophia Jex-Blake and the pioneers of the Lady Doctors' movement, were, it would seem on looking back, scarcely so mildly mannered, so peacefully inclined as those who now sit placidly beside 'the sweet girl graduates' of our day, on the class-room benches, and acknowledge the reign of the lady doctor as an accomplished fact. A torchlight procession of modern times is apparently a cheerful and picturesque function, smiled on by the authorities, and welcomed as a rather unique means of doing honour to a new Lord Rector or some famous guest of the city or the University. In Mr Stevenson's time, a torchlight procession had all the joys of 'forbidden fruit' to the merry lads who braved the police and the professors for the pleasure of marching through the streets to the final bonfire on the Calton Hill, from the scrimmage round which they emerged with clothes well oiled and singed, and faces and hands as black as much besmearing could make them ; while anxious friends at home trembled lest a night in the police cells should be the reward of the ringleaders.

Of one such procession, in the spring when Mr Stevenson's law studies were first interrupted by a journey south for his health, a clever student wrote an epic which was presented to me by one of Louis Stevenson's Balfour cousins as something *very precious !* The occasion was the Duke of Edinburgh's wedding, in 1874, and, yellow and faded, the *Epic* still graces my *Every Day Book,* and, as one reads its inspiriting lines, one sees again those bygone days in which the slim figure and eager face of Louis Stevenson are always so conspicuous in every memory of the old, grey city of his birth.

The following lines from the clever skit give a really excellent picture of the college life in his day.

> . . . 'A deputation we
> Sent hither by the students to demand
> That they—that is the students—in a band
> May march, illumed by torches flaring bright,
> Along the leading streets on Friday night.
> Brave was the Provost, yet towards his heart
> The glowing life blood thrilled with sudden start ;
> Well might he tremble at the name he heard,
> The Students ! Kings might tremble at the word !
> He thought of all the terrors of the past,
> Of that fell row in Blackie's, April last—
> Of Simpson wight, and Stirling-Maxwell too,
> Of Miss Jex-Blake and all her lovely crew—
> He thought, " If thus these desperadoes dare
> To act with ladies, learned, young and fair,

Old women, like the Councillors and me,
To direr torments still reserved may be.
The better part of valour is discretion,
I'll try to soften them by prompt concession."
Then coughing thrice, impression due to make
And clear his throat, in accents mild he spake,
"Ye have my leave, 'V.R.,' I mean 'D.V.'"
The students bowed, retired, and he was free.'

The High Sheriff and the Chief of Police, when they heard of the Provost's weakness, were filled with wrath and dismay, and very promptly insisted on his lordship taking back the concession, so that this historic procession was as much 'forbidden fruit' as its predecessors, and the students probably enjoyed it the more that they had as usual to dare all those in authority to carry it out.

Another old-time enjoyment of that date was a snow-ball fight. Whether snow is less plentiful, or students are too cultured and too refined for these rough pastimes it is impossible to say, but certain it is that a really *great* snow-ball fight is also a thing of the past. In those days they were Homeric combats, and a source of keen enjoyment to Robert Louis Stevenson, a very funny account of whom, on one of these occasions, was given me at the time by his cousin, Lewis Balfour, from Leven, himself a jovial medical student enjoying an active part in the melée. On the occasion of a great battle in the winter of 1869—or 1870—Mr Stevenson and one or two men, now well known in various professions, had seated them-selves on a ledge in the quadrangle to watch the fight. From this vantage ground they encouraged the com-batants, but took no active part in the fray. Within swarmed the students armed with snowballs, without, the lads of the town, equally active, stormed the gates. All were too intent on the battle to notice the advent of the police, who rushed into the college quadrangle and made prisoners where they could. Craning his neck too much, in his keen enjoyment, Mr Stevenson overbalanced himself, slipped from his perch and was promptly captured by 'a bobby,' and, in spite of gallant efforts for his rescue, was ignominiously marched off to the Police Office at the very moment that his blandly unconscious mother was driving up the Bridges. It was useless for his attendant friends to assert that he had been a non-combatant. Was he not taken in the very thick of the fight? The police had him and they meant to keep him for he could not produce sufficient bail from his somewhat empty pockets. His cousin and his friends, by leaving all their stray coins, their watches and other valuables, managed to secure his release so that he had not the experience—which it is possible he might have enjoyed—of passing a night in the police cells of his native city.

In his introduction to the *Memoirs of Professor Fleeming-Jenkin*, he himself tells a good story of his relations with that Professor, who was always a true and appreciative friend to his clever if idle student. He had handed in so few cards at the class of Engineering that his certificate was not forthcoming until he told his friend that his father would be very vexed if he could not produce the certificate—which he never intended to *use*— whereat the tender-hearted Professor handed it to him.

Another prime favourite of his among the Professors was Professor Kelland; and one can well understand the attraction which the dainty, gentle refinement of that most

kind-hearted of men had for a nature so akin to it as
young Stevenson's. All Professor Kelland's students
loved him ; this one understood him also. Professor
Masson was one of the giants of those days whom he
was also most capable of appreciating, and whose lectures
he occasionally attended although not a member of his
class ; and, himself not without his amiable eccentricities,
he could not fail to have a soft spot in his heart for the
quaint humour and the pleasant eccentricity which en-
deared Professor Blackie to his class and to the public.
He was a poor attender at the Greek Class, however, and
when he presented himself for his certificate the keen blue
eyes of the Professor looked at him critically, and the
Professor's remark was that he had been so seldom
present at lectures it was hardly possible to recognise
his face !

Many of the students of that day have taken a good
place in the world ; some of them have long ere now left
the things of time behind them ; one or two of them Mr
Stevenson has pictured in his graphic pages. Several of
them regarded him as an interesting personality, but very
few of them suspected that he was ' the chiel amang them
takin' notes ' for future work that would bring world-wide
fame, not only to himself, but to his University and to the
city of his birth.

On the 2nd March 1869 he was proposed by George
Melville, Esq., Advocate, as a member of the Speculative
Society, and we know from *Memories and Portraits* how
much he appreciated his membership of that Society,
which has in its day included in the roll, on which his
name stood No. 992, most of the men whose names are

honoured in Scotland's capital, and many of whom the fame and the memory are revered in far places of the earth. That he might smoke in the hall of the Speculative, in the very stronghold of University authority, he playfully professes to have been his chief pleasure in the thing; but other men, to whom his earnest face, his eagerness in debate, made one of the pleasures of its meetings, tell another story, and it was commonly said in those days that there would always be something of interest in hand if Stevenson took a part in it.

When he forsook the profession of engineering, Mr Stevenson attended the Law classes at the University, with the intention of being called to the Bar, but it is not on record that he was a more exemplary student of law than he had been of engineering, and he still found more satisfaction in his truant rambles and his meditations in old graveyards than he did in the legitimate study of his profession.

CHAPTER IV

AS I FIRST KNEW HIM

'Blessed are his parents in a son, so graced in face and figure
And of mind so wise.'
—LORD DERBY'S TRANSLATION OF *The Iliad*.

THAT was one of the quotations by which in those days we were wont to describe Mr Stevenson. Strictly speaking, perhaps he was not a handsome man. He was too slim, too ethereal, if one may use the term, to attain to anything sufficiently commonplace to be described as merely handsome. But he was indeed 'graced in face and figure,' for he possessed that rare attribute *distinction*, and his face, with its wonderfully luminous eyes, its ever changing expression, had a beauty peculiar to itself, and one which harmonised perfectly with the quaint wisdom of his mind.

That wisdom was so deep, yet so whimsical, so peculiar and so many-sided that one can only apply to its possessor another quotation half indignantly thrown at him, when he was too successful in argument, by an acquaintance of his, whose quick wit had a great charm for him.

'We gaze and still the wonder grows
That one small head can carry all he knows.'

He bowed to the compliment, he demurred as to the smallness of his head, and he enjoyed the quotation immensely. With the same opponent he once tried a competition in verse-making. Both showed considerable skill, but the umpire decided that Louis had won, so he bore off in triumph the prize of a bottle of olives, and was only sorry that he could not compel the loser to share his feast, which he well knew would be as abhorrent to her as it was delightful to him.

With Edinburgh, wind-swept and grey, with its biting breeze, its swirling dust of March, there will always be associated in my mind certain memories of Robert Louis Stevenson, and of that happy home of the Stevenson family, 17 Heriot Row. In summer sunshine Swanston, lying cosily at the foot of the Pentlands, claimed them year by year, but every winter found them, for business or pleasure, established in that most homelike house, the windows of which, to the front, looked into the Heriot Row gardens, and at the back, from that upper flat where was the book-lined study of the son of the house, snatched a glimpse, over roofs and chimney cans, of the gold-fringed shores of Fife.

Across the blue Forth in Fife, at the little seaside town of Leven, well known to golfing fame, there had settled in 1866 an uncle of R. L. Stevenson, Dr John Balfour, who was noted for his gallantry and skill throughout the Indian Mutiny, and in more than one outbreak of cholera in India and at home. Of the town and the man Mr Stevenson gives a graphic picture in *Random Memories*, when describing a visit to the Fife coast, where his father was making an inspection of lights and harbours.

In 1849 when home on leave Dr Balfour volunteered to go to Davidson's Mains, in the parish of Cramond,

where as a specialist in cholera symptoms he was amazed
to find the outbreak as virulent and as fatal as the
Asiatic cholera he had seen in India. In 1866, when
another wave of cholera swept over Britain, he was asked
to go to Slateford, where he coped with its ravages almost
single-handed, saving life in every case after he went,
except those already too far gone before his arrival.
In late autumn of the same year the scourge broke
out seriously in the small towns on the coast of
Fife, and Dr Balfour went to Leven, where the
doctor had just died of it, and a state of panic pre-
vailed, and there too he succeeded in quickly stamping
it out.

Having retired from his Indian appointment he felt
idle time hang heavy on hand, so he acceded to the
request of the inhabitants and went to Leven to take
up practice there. His wife, who was a cousin of his
own, and their four children, shortly after followed him
from Edinburgh, and he built a house called 'The Turret'
there, where he remained until his greatly lamented death
in 1886.

There from childhood I grew up in intimate friendship
with the young Balfours, and went out and in to the
doctor's house, receiving in it such kindness from parents
and children that it was regarded by me as a second
home, and its inmates were looked upon as one's 'ain
folk.' As one's 'ain folk,' too, by-and-bye, were regarded those other Balfour families, notably Dr George
W. Balfour's household and Miss Balfour, and the
nephews and nieces who had their home with her—who
made of the little Fife town their holiday resort. Later

an Edinburgh school and long visits to Edinburgh relatives made the Scotch capital as familiar to me as Fife;
and then the Stevenson family in their home at Heriot
Row were added to the little circle of friends, now, alas!
so thinned by grievous blanks.   Old and young have
passed into 'The Silent Land,' and life is infinitely
the poorer for those severed friendships—those lost re-
gards of early days.

Not a few of the old folk were notable in their time,
some of the younger generation have made, or mean to
make, some stir in the world.   But round none of them
gathers so much of romance of honour and of distinction
as about Robert Louis Stevenson, who used to visit his
uncle's house in Leven, doubtless from one of those
expeditions to Anstruther, of which he tells us that he
spent his time by day in giving a perfunctory attention to
the harbour at which his father's firm were working, and
lived his real life by night scribbling romances in his
lodgings.   It is on record that he felt a thrill of well-
merited pride when an Anstruther small boy pointed
to him, as he stood beside the workmen, and said:
'There's the man that's takin' charge.'   But he assuredly knew more of pleasure in his hours of scribbling
than in his hours of attendance at the works, although
the out-of-door, wind-swept part of engineering was never
so abhorrent to him as office work.   In the office he was
known very little; but tradition has it that a small pile
of evil spellings is still treasured there as a characteristic
memento of the genius, and the thought has been known
to comfort the sad hearts of other apprentice engineers
afflicted with a like shakiness in their orthography, that

the now much appreciated man of letters once shared their melancholy failing.

Stories of all sorts were handed about in our little clique of the wondrous Robert Louis whose sayings and doings were already precious to an appreciative circle of relatives and friends. But it was not till sometime in the autumn of 1869 that he first became personally known to me.

The introduction took place on a September afternoon in the drawing-room of 'The Turret,' and he inspired a great deal of awe in a youthful admirer who even then had literary aspirations, and who therefore looked up to him with much respect as someone who already wrote. From that time he was regarded as one of the quaintest, the most original and the most charming personalities among one's acquaintances. There was about him, in those days, a whimsical affectation, a touch of purely delightful vanity that never wholly left him in later life, and that far from repelling, as it would have done in any one more commonplace, was so intrinsically a part of his artistic nature that it was rather attractive than otherwise Full of delightful humour, his idlest sayings—when he took the trouble to say anything which he frequently did not!—were teeming with the elements not only of laughter but of thought, and you wondered, long after you had talked with him, why it was that you saw new lights on things, and found food for mirth and matter for reflection where neither had suggested itself before.

In those days he was not only original himself, but he had to a great degree that rare faculty of bringing to the surface in others the very smallest spark of originality,

and of remembering it and appreciating it in a way that
was stimulating and helpful to those who had the
pleasure of knowing him.   When the little seaside town
was empty of visitors, and it was not time to pay Edinburgh visits for the season, in February and March, one
kindness of his was very greatly prized by some of us
who beguiled the tedium of the winter months by writing
for and conducting an amateur magazine, called *Ours*.
For this, in 1872 and 1873, Mr Stevenson gave us a
short contribution, *The Nun of Aberhuern*, a trifle in
his own graceful style, which, as he was even then beginning to be known in the world of letters, we valued
much.   Moreover, he took a friendly interest in the
sheets of blue MS. paper so closely written over with our
somewhat juvenile productions, and made here a criticism,
there a prediction, which has not been without its effect
on the future work of some of us.

Mr Stevenson was always kind and always sympathetic ;
he laughed at your follies of course, but he did it so
pleasantly that the laughter seemed almost a compliment,
and the kindness was more memorable than the mirth.   In
one among his juniors at least, imbued like himself with a
love of old-time romance and of ancient story, he inspired
a passion of gratitude that abides to this day.   Mr Stevenson not only never laughed, as the other boys and girls did,
nor treated the memory of delightful childish plays with con-
tempt, as was the fashion of the generation just grown up,
he never even smiled over the unfeminine tastes of a child
who went pirate-hunting in an upturned table with a towel
for a sail and dried orange skins for provender—or whose
dolls were not treated as those dainty girlish playthings

ought to be, as pretty babies and gay society dames, but figured as the tattered and battered followers of Prince Charlie—himself a hero very much the worse for the wear in a plaid and a kilt!—after Culloden. Or, in gayer moods, the same dolls attended his receptions at Holyrood in garish garments, or masqueraded as Mary Queen of Scots and her four Maries in that 'turret chamber high of ancient Holyrood' where 'she summoned Rizzio with his lute and bade the minstrel play.'

Mr Stevenson listened gravely to all these things. He professed a real interest in them. He even remembered the names of the puppets and the parts they had played, and so gained for himself an enduring niche in the heart that had bitterly resented the mockery of the others. It is quite possible that a nature so gentle and so appreciative as his really *felt* the sympathy. The juniors are rarely mistaken as to the genuineness of the feelings of their elders, and his interest certainly rang true to the youthful mind. He had been himself a delicate child, so he was capable of understanding how many weary and solitary hours the romantic plays had filled pleasantly.

It is not a memory of much moment, perhaps, but it shows that even at an age when most young men are too keenly concerned with themselves and their own affairs to take much trouble for those who are a few years their juniors, Mr Stevenson had thought and sympathy to spare for the small joys and sorrows, the interests, and the 'make-believes' that had amused a lonely child, and which, after all, in one form or another, make up a good deal of life to most of us.

One is inclined to gather from his books, and from the

statements accredited to him in magazines and news-
papers, that he never took women very seriously. He
may not have done so—save those who were very near
and dear to him, and they were set in a sacred shrine of
their own—but he certainly always treated women very
charmingly ; and the young girl relatives and friends, who
were accustomed to be much in his home circle, had
never any reason to complain of the lack of the most
dainty and courtly attentions or of a most constant and
spontaneous kindness from the somewhat solemn youth,
who, like other youths of twenty, considered that it
showed a great knowledge of the world to affect a
rather cynical disdain of the feminine half of humanity.
In himself there was, curiously enough, always a reminder
of the feminine ; an almost girlish look passed now and
again, in those days, over the thin delicately-tinted face,
and a womanly gentleness in voice and manner reminded
one of his mother.

The same ready sympathy, the same power, as it were,
of putting himself into a friend's place and entering with
heart and soul into the affairs of others which made him
so interested a listener to a young girl's story of her
childhood's plays, made him in his later years the friend
of the Samoans, the champion of Samoan liberties, and,
all through his life, the one man whom the men and
women who knew him loved with the love that is only
given to the very few, and those the few, too often, whose
death in life's prime, or before it, prove them to have
been among those whom the old poet tells us 'the gods
love.'

Nothing at this time was more remarkable in Mr

Stevenson than his extraordinary youthfulness of mind.
At an age when other young men affect to be blasé and
world weary he was delightfully and fearlessly boyish.
Boyish even in his occasional half-comic solemnity of
appearance ; he was boyish likewise in his charming jests
and jokes, and, above all, in his hearty delight in any
outdoor ' ploy ' that came in his way.

A comical instance of this nearness of the boy to the
surface in him displayed itself one grey east-windy afternoon at Leven, when one saw quite another side to him
than the literary and dilettante one displayed, with something of a mannered affectation, the day before in ' The
Turret ' drawing-room. He had walked down to the
sands with his aunt and there were assembled various
younger members of the Balfour clique, and some whom
age and sex ought perhaps to have taught to despise,
though it had not, the hoydenish pleasures of ' a sea-
house.' A ' sea-house,' for the benefit of the uninitiated,
is a deep hole dug in the sand while the tide is out, and
the sand taken from the hole is built round in broad, high
walls to make the fort resist as long as possible the rush
of the incoming waves. It takes hours to make, but no
trouble is too great, for is there not the fierce joy of
adventure at the last when the waves finally win in the
struggle and the huddled-together inmates of the now
submerged house are thoroughly soaked with spray and
salt water ?

The ' sea-house,' the shouts of its builders, the tempt-
ing curl on the waves, as each one came a little further,
the slight rise of the wind driving the breakers hurriedly
landwards, were evidently too much for Mr Stevenson.

One moment the weight of his nineteen years and the duty of politeness to his aunt restrained him, the next Mrs Balfour was left standing alone, and overcome with laughter, while Louis was in the sea-house scolding, praising, and exhorting all at once, but above all imploring us to 'sit it out a little longer' as wave after wave widened the breach in the ramparts of sand, and

> ' In every hole the sea came up,
> Till it could come no more,'

while wetter and wetter grew the heroic few who, with Mr Stevenson 'sat it out' loyally, till it was possible to sit there no longer. Then wet—wetter indeed than ever before—the remnant crept home to be frowned upon and punished but to know no repentance ; for had not Robert Louis been the ringleader, and was there any punishment invented that could take from the joy and the pride of a mischievous adventure in which *he* had had a part! And he, with the water dripping from his trousers and 'squirching' in his boots, was perfectly and placidly happy, regardless of his aunt's dismay and the future horrors of a possible bad cold. He had been a schoolboy again for the all too brief half hour beside the grey and gurly sea, and that youthfulness, that survived through all the patient suffering of his life and that seems to laugh out of the pages of his books to the last, was in the ascendant as he walked off jauntily townwards, amiably oblivious of the lecture his aunt gave him by the way.

Anything which brought him into close contact with the sea had a charm for him, even that mock combat with the waves of the autumn equinox on the flat shore of Fife. Therefore at this time although classes and study were a weariness to him his days spent in the old-fashioned town of Anstruther, or on the desolate coast of Caithness, had many pleasures; had many romances also, for everywhere he went he picked up odd and out-of-the-way knowledge, and came across strange stories and stranger characters, from the lingering tradition of the poor relic of the Spanish Armada, the Duke of Modena Sidonia,* who after his sojourn in Fair Isle landed at Anstruther and still glorified the quaint sea-port in the East Neuk with his ghostly dignity—to the peer of the realm, in actual flesh and blood, whom Mr Stevenson found acting as a home missionary to the present day population of the Fair Isle. All things were treasured in the note-book of his memory, or jotted down in the note-book in his pocket; and, while the engineer progressed very little in his profession, the future novelist was undergoing a training for his work almost perfect in its way and assuredly most admirably suited to the nature that loved an open air life and revelled in an existence on the sea or beside it.

Possibly not all aspiring civil engineers, certainly very few budding novelists, so test the reality of things as to go down into the ocean depths in a diver's dress and in the company of a professional diver, but this Robert Louis Stevenson actually did. His account of it, in bygone days, was gruesomely graphic, his pen-and-ink sketch of it, to be read in *Random Memories*, is not

---

* Although Mr Stevenson spoke and wrote of this personage as 'the Duke of Modena Sidonia,' he was in reality Don Jan Gomez de Modena, who is mentioned in T. M'Crie's ' Life of Andrew Melville.'

less so; and the thing itself must have been an experience well worth having to a mind like his. Well worth knowing too, both to the man and to the future creator of character, were those brave hardy sons of toil who did the rough work of his firm's harbours and lighthouses; and many a good yarn he must have heard them spin as he stood side by side with them on some solid block of granite, or on some outlying headland, or chatted and smoked with the captain and the sailors of *The Pharos* as she made her rounds among the islands.

CHAPTER V

HOME LIFE

'O, pleasant party round the fire.'
—R. L. STEVENSON.

OFTEN a little indifferent, sometimes politely bored in general society, it was at home that Robert Louis Stevenson seemed to me to be seen to the greatest advantage. That little household of three, that delightful trio who so thoroughly appreciated each other were charming everywhere, but only quite perfect when taken together within the hospitable walls that enshrined so true a home. Not a house or an abiding place merely, whence the business or the gaieties of life could be comfortably indulged in, but a *home* where, however much the amusements of the Scotch capital were shared in and appreciated, the truest happiness lay around the quiet fireside where the mother, father, and son loved and understood each other with a love the deeper, that the intense Scotch reticence of all made it, like a hidden jewel, the more precious because so rarely displayed to strangers' eyes.

No son could be more fortunate in his parents, no parents could have given a child a more unselfish devotion, a more comprehending sympathy. His very delicacy and

57

the anxiety it had so often caused them had drawn their hearts more tenderly to him, and, absolutely happy in each other, they were equally happy in their pride and pleasure in their son's evident genius and most original personality.

In days when discontent and extravagance have done so much to lessen, at least upon the surface of things, the sacredness of home, and weaken the solemnity of marriage, it is comforting and pleasant to look back upon such a home as that was, and to realise that it is possible, in the midst of a busy life of work and of pleasure, to preserve an inner holy of holies around the domestic hearth, into which no jarring discord, no paltry worldly worry, can come, because love is there. Before love's clear gaze all that is selfish and petty and false dies away, while all that is true, good, and gentle makes for sweet peace and that perfect union of hearts which can alone create a true marriage and a perfect home life.

Into the Stevenson household, as into other households, came from time to time real worry, real grief, and not infrequent anxiety. The very frailty of tenure by which their son had always held his life was in itself a daily burden to the parents. Mrs Stevenson, especially in her earlier married life, was often far from strong ; to Mr Stevenson came now and then those darker moods to which the Scotch temperament, particularly when tinged with the Celtic, is liable. Personal and business disappointments were not wholly unknown, although life in these latter respects was one saved at least from monetary anxieties, and crowned with a large measure of success. But in " all the changes and chances of this mortal life "

this household had a sure sheet anchor on which to de-
pend. Love met the trials smiling, and because they loved
each other they were clothed in the armour of defence.

It was a home ennobled by a high ideal of what life
ought to be, and hallowed by a strong and personal
faith in God. Mr Stevenson's somewhat austere Calvinism
gave a gravity to his character and his religion that were
admirably balanced by the happy nature and the sunny
active faith of his wife, whose religion was none the less
real and earnest that it was bright and always cheerfully
practical. Both loved the grand old Church of Scotland,
with her far-reaching history and her noble traditions;
both, with money and personal interest, helped not only
their own congregations of Greenside and St Stephen's but the
missions and schemes of the Church at large, and many
private kindnesses and public charities besides evinced
their liberality of heart. Mrs Stevenson, among other
things, took a keen pleasure in work for the Indian
Zenanas, and among his many engrossments Mr Stevenson
was greatly occupied as to the public good of Edinburgh,
and notably interested himself in the restoration of St
Giles, that grand old landmark of national history of
which, in its present condition, Scotland has every reason
to be proud.

In such a home as this Robert Louis Stevenson was
from early childhood educated in a deeply-rooted respect
for the Bible and the old solemn teachings which gave to
Scotland those 'graves of the martyrs,' of which he so
often writes. The Calvinism of his ancestors, inherited
to a certain extent by his father, softened to him by his
mother's sweetness of nature and brightness of faith, always

remained with him something to be regarded with a tender
reverence; and if, as he grew to manhood, the 'modern
spirit' changed and modified his beliefs, so that it might
be said of him, as of so many large natures and earnest
souls,

'His God he cabins not in creeds,'

God and religion remained very real to him; and the
high ideal of duty first learned in his childhood's home
guided his life to the last. Robert Fergusson's life and
poems interested him greatly, and he often declared himself drawn to him by a certain spiritual affinity; while,
when suffering from his frequent attacks of distressing
illness, he sometimes thought with dread of Fergusson's
sad fate.

Pleasure as well as duty, however, was always made
welcome in the Stevenson home. Mr and Mrs Thomas
Stevenson held no stern views of everyday life, no gayer
or brighter household could be found than theirs. None
certainly existed where young folk received a warmer
welcome, whether the family were established for the
winter at 17 Heriot Row, or were spending the summer
at Swanston, that delightful nook, nestling in the shelter
of the Pentland hills, where the old-fashioned flowers had
so sweet a scent, the rustic sounds of country life were so
full of charming music, and where the home trio themselves loved

'Every path and every plot,
Every bush of roses,
Every blue forget-me-not
Where the dew reposes.'

Differing much in their natures, but fitting, as it
were, closely into each other's souls and characters,

Louis Stevenson's parents early made for him that ideal
of home and of marriage that shows itself from the first
in his writings, just here a line and there a sentence,
which indicates how his thoughts ran, and how, whatever
enjoyment he might take in poking cynicism at women in
the abstract, he was full of a noble idea, a manly longing
for that one woman, of whose soul and his own, he could
say—

> ' Once and beyond recollection,
>   Once ere the skies were unfurled,
>   These an immortal affection
>   Found at the birth of the world,'

a woman who would be what his mother was to his
father, a something as sacred as all through his life that
mother was to him. Save that Mrs Thomas Stevenson's
eyes were rather hazel than blue, it might have been of
her that the late Professor Blackie wrote so sweetly :—

> ' True to herself and to the high ideal
>   That God's grace gave her to inform the real,
>   True to her kind, and to your every feeling
>   Respondent with a power of kindliest healing
>   She knows no falseness, even the courtliest lie ;
>   She dreams not, truth flows from her deep blue eye,
>   And if her tongue speaks pleasant things to all,
>   'Tis that she loveth well both great and small,
>   And all in her that mortals call politeness
>   Is but the image of her bright soul's brightness.'

That Stevenson home was to many of us, besides the
son of the house, a picture of what a true life ought to
be, and one that seemed to make the realisation of all
high ideals possible in whatever fashion one's own existence might ultimately be led.

There was something so strong and manly in Mr Thomas Stevenson, something so sweetly womanly in his wife. A beautiful woman always, because hers was the beauty of soul, as well as of feature, in those early seventies, one cannot imagine anyone more graceful, more gracious, or more charming than she was.

It would also be difficult to imagine a wife or mother more sympathetic or more sensible. She could always see the fun of things ; she never objected to clubs and men's dinners, and the excuse for a night away from the home hearth, that is so dear to the best of men.

Not many weeks before her death, when we were talking of those happy days of long ago, she told me that she always took a book and contented herself, and then was ready to be interested when the truant returned with a latch-key. An example, that if closely followed, would assuredly make for domestic peace. And one fancies that the woman who said smilingly, she always much approved of ' The Evening Club,' because her husband or son could make merry there so late, that she was sound asleep, and could not miss their conversation, was likely to be a pleasant wife to live with, and an ideal mother for a son of such Bohemian tendencies as Robert Louis.

Even that marvellous taste in dress which her son affected, and which would certainly have dismayed more conventional mothers, only amused her immensely. Among other jottings of hers about him in her little note-book is one which relates with much appreciation that a faithful servant says of him, ' One summer he tried to wear a frock-coat and tall hat, but after a little he laid them aside and said, " I am not going to be a swell any more," and returned to the velveteen coat and the straw hat which he preferred.'

Except at a wedding, or some such solemn function, whereat he probably looked misery personified, one cannot remember him so conventionally apparelled as in the frock-coat and the tall hat. Possibly it was before this access of propriety temporarily had him in its grasp that one day we saw him in Princes Street 'taking the air' in an open cab with a Stevenson cousin, attired in like manner with himself. In those days fashionable people often walked in Princes Street in the afternoon, so what was our dismay, in the midst of quite a crowd of the gay world, to see that open cab, at a word of command from Robert Louis, draw near the pavement as we approached, when two battered straw hats were lifted to us with quite a Parisian grace. Both young men wore sailor hats with brilliant ribbon bands, both were attired in flannel cricketing jackets with broad bright stripes, and round Louis's neck was knotted a huge yellow silk handkerchief, while over both their heads one of them held an open umbrella. In days when the wearing of cricketing clothes, except in the playing fields, was in Scotland still so uncommon that it is on authentic record that an elderly unmarried lady in an east coast watering place, on meeting in its high street a young man in boating flannels, was so shocked at the innovation that she promptly went home, leaving all her shopping undone and her tea-drinking and friendly gossip forgotten, such an apparition as that in the open cab required more courage to face than people accustomed to the present-day use of gay tennis garb can easily imagine. It was

fortunate that nerve to return the salutation smilingly was
not wanting, or Mr Stevenson would certainly have piti-
lessly chaffed the timid victims of conventionality afterwards.

Having borne the ordeal with such courage as we
possessed, we hastened to have tea with Mrs Stevenson,
whose first question was, ' Have you seen Lou ? '

And when we described that startling vision that was
slowly creeping along Princes Street in the open cab, she
laughed till her tears fell.   In half an hour or so her son
came in cool and unconcerned, and as punctiliously polite
as if his attire had been the orthodox apparel for an
afternoon tea-party.

The effects of his dressing and appearance on the
foreign mind is most humorously described by himself
in his *Epilogue to an Inland Voyage*, where the extraordinary nature of his garments so dismayed the French
police that while his friend, the late Sir Walter G. Simpson,
' The Cigarette,' was allowed to go free, ' The Arethusa '
was popped into prison, kept there for an hour or two,
and finally hustled off to Paris, an adventure of the
two friends, who were so systematically taken for ' bag-
men,' on that charming expedition, which was always told
with much laughter by ' The Arethusa's ' parents.

One of the last memories of Mr Stevenson in Edinburgh that distinctly remains with me was finding him
looking into the window of Messrs Douglas & Foulis
in Castle Street on a grey, east windy day that was cold
enough to make the thickest great-coat necessary.   But
he was visibly shivering in one of his favourite short
velvet coats.   It was palpably too short in the arms, and

certainly the worse for wear ; his long hair fell almost to his shoulders, and he wore a Tyrolese hat of soft felt. With a whimsical and appreciative glance at his garments, he offered to accompany me along Princes Street ; so we set off westwards together, when, so charming was his conversation, that long before we reached the doorsteps of his relative's house, which was my destination, one had forgotten that the wind was in the east, and the sky greyer than the pavements, and only longed for the walk to begin over again, that he might talk all the way. These eccentricities of attire were merely a part of the rather attractive vanity of a clever youth, whose exuberance of spirits was, in spite of much bad health, at that time so great that he was often merry with a gaiety that was as child-like as it was. amusing. In later life he gradually modified his ideas as to dress, and in the *Vailima Letters* he writes of himself in Samoa as going to Apia to social amusements in most orthodox coats and ties.

At evening parties he always looked like a martyr in the dismal black coat and white tie, which he described as a mixture of the livery of a waiter and the mourning of an undertaker. At dances, he propped himself against a wall, in a doorway or in some coign of vantage about the staircase, looking limp and miserable, but keenly observant all the time. When he found a congenial soul, whether man or woman, to talk to, he brightened, the limpness vanished, and his quick flow of wit and fancy streamed on in a delightful river of talk which touched on grave and gay with equal ease, and was exactly what a poet describes, as—

> ' His talk was like a stream that runs
> With rapid change from rocks to roses,
> It skipped from politics to puns,
> It passed from Mahomet to Moses.
> Beginning with the laws that keep
> The planets in their rapid courses,
> And ending with a precept deep
> For stewing eels or shoeing horses.'

Although he looked so unhappy at dances or 'at homes,' at dinners, if the guests were fitly chosen, he was thoroughly at his ease and exceedingly amusing. With his few intimate friends too he was seen at his best; but in general society he was usually as bored as he looked.

The Edinburgh of that day was very pleasant socially. Its world seemed somewhat smaller than it is now, less ostentatiously rich, more seriously cultured; or so at least it appeared to the young folk who belonged to the old-fashioned law and professional set in which the Stevensons largely had their acquaintance. People in that set still lived, more than they do to-day, eastwards or northwards of Heriot Row, in the large old houses which were so homelike and so comfortable. The centre of things was in those grand grey houses from Heriot Row upwards to Charlotte Square, westwards to Randolph Cliff and a little way over the Dean Bridge. Drumsheugh Gardens was an innovation. The terraces, Royal, Regent, and Carlton, that 'west end of the east,' were still fashionable, and few people had, as yet, migrated southwards to

> ' That proud part of Morningside,
> Where houses girt with gardens
> Do stretch down far and wide.'

It was not a very large world, but it was a very agreeable one, and one which had its notabilities. Lord Neaves with his delightful songs, and the other old-time judges were still with us. Sir David Brewster was not so very long dead ; Sir James Y. Simpson was yet a very recent memory. Professor Blackie was in the zenith of his fame. Sir Daniel Macnee told his wonderful stories ; Professor, now Sir, Douglas Maclagan sang his delightful songs. Mr Sam Bough's hearty laugh rang out among the artists, and Sir R. Christison, and Syme, and Keith, and Lister, had made the Edinburgh medical world famous. Professors Masson, Tait, Kelland, Crum-Brown, Fleeming-Jenkin— in whose theatricals R. L. Stevenson took a picturesque part—and a host of other well-known names were among the guests at dinners, and most beloved personality of all, perhaps, Dr John Brown, accompanied by his 'doggies' still nodded to us out of his carriage window, or left wonderful scraps of drawings on the hall tables as he passed out from seeing a patient. And everywhere in that pleasant world the Stevenson family were welcome and well known.

By the host of young people who are now in turn taking the busy work of life, from which so many of the elders are resting for ever, parties at 17 Heriot Row and at Swanston were much appreciated. Dinner parties for young people were not then so common as now, and the delightful ones given by Mr and Mrs Thomas Stevenson were greatly enjoyed. The guests were carefully chosen, and limited to ten or twelve, so that conversation at dinner was general. And how amusing that conversation was ! The humour of father and son as they drew each other out was wonderful, they capped each other's good things, and somehow made less gifted folk shine in the conversation also in a way peculiar to them and which was fully shared by Mrs Thomas Stevenson, who made the most charming of hostesses. Father and son on these occasions were simply full of jests and jollity, everything started an argument, and every argument lent itself to fun. It is odd that nothing definite of those clever sayings of theirs seems to return to one; it is only, as it were, the memory of an aroma that filled the air sweetly at the time, and is still faintly present with one that remains; the actual 'bon-mots' have unhappily passed away. It is consoling to find that Mr Edmund Gosse, who in *Kit-Cats* writes delightfully of his friend Louis Stevenson, notes the same intangible character of his talk.

After the little dinners there were delightful informal dances, to which nephews, nieces, friends, and neighbours came as well as the dinner guests, and one can still remember with a smile, perilously near to tears, Mr Thomas Stevenson driving his unwilling son to dance the old-time dance 'Sir Roger de Coverley,' which the elder man loved and the younger professed to scorn even while he entered with a zeal that finally satisfied his father into the performance of it, that always ended an informal evening at 17 Heriot Row.

Music, too, was a pleasant feature of those little parties, and one still recalls, especially, the songs and the lovely voice of a favourite niece of Mrs Stevenson, whose early death made the first break in the home at 'The Turret,' too soon to be followed by the passing away of all save one of that happy household. Even now, after the lapse of so many years, one seems to see Mr Thomas Stevenson leaning eagerly forward as she sang such sweet old songs as ' My Mother bids me bind my Hair,' and 'She wore a wreath of Roses,' or Robert Louis applauding his favourites, ' I shot an Arrow into the Air,' and ' The Sea hath its Pearls.'

On one occasion one of these merry parties was enlivened by the presence of some young Japanese engineer students, who were on tour in Edinburgh, and who had brought introductions to the distinguished engineer, who made them very cordially welcome. It was not then very common to meet Japanese, and these quiet dignified young men, in their gracefully flowing black garments, interested the Stevenson family and their youthful guests greatly.

CHAPTER VI

HIS CHOICE OF A LITERARY LIFE AND HIS EARLIER BOOKS

'A clerk foredoom'd his father's soul to cross,
Who pens a stanza when he should engross.'
—POPE'S *Epistle to Dr Arbuthnot.*

His son's refusal to become a civil engineer, and to take his natural position in the family business, was undoubtedly a great trial to a man of Mr Thomas Stevenson's character and professional traditions. That business had in it not only wealth, honour, and success, but, to every Stevenson, the glamour of romance, the fascination of adventure, and to the father his firm's history appealed strongly. Therefore the blow that fell upon him during that memorable walk, when his son at last found courage to confess to him that he could not persevere in the traditional path which he was expected to tread, must have been a crushing one, and it said much for the strength of his fatherly affection that he received it as he did. It was a painful decision for the son to make, and an equally painful one for the parents to hear.

Mrs Thomas Stevenson as well as her husband felt it a keen disappointment that her son could not walk in his father's footsteps. To them, as to all parents of their position and very natural social prejudices, it seemed a foolish thing for a man to turn seriously to literature as a means of winning his daily bread. The Edinburgh of that day did not think much of the profession of letters, and although the memory of Sir Walter Scott, the 'Edinburgh Reviewers,' and the literary lights of an earlier time was still green, all parents held the opinion that, although a few authors had made for themselves fame and fortune, literature was but a beggarly trade at the best, and one to which no wise man would apprentice his son.

Only those who knew the elder Mr Stevenson's nature well could fully understand how great a trial to him was his son's decision ; and only those very near and dear to him could quite appreciate the depth of the father's love, the tenderness of the father's heart, which permitted no tinge of bitterness, no lasting shadow of repining, to darken his relations with his son or to lessen in the slightest his overwhelming affection for him. Sensitive in the extreme, the son in his turn could not fail to feel his father's dis- appointment, almost to exaggerate its effect on the older man in his own tender-hearted remorse that he was unable to fulfil his destiny in any other way than by following litera- ture, which was calling him with no uncertain voice. It was good, therefore, to hear from the lips of the wife and mother, who was so fully in the confidence of both, that no abiding cloud remained between the father and the son, and that both quietly accepted the inevitable when law, like engineering, was also laid aside to allow Louis to fulfil his one strong desire. Lovingly and unselfishly the parents finally accepted the fact that genius must have its way, and that in the dainty book-lined study, in travel by ways quaint and unusual, in prolonged sojourns in search of health in distant lands, the younger Stevenson's life-work was to be done.

When he found that his son would not be an engineer, Mr Thomas Stevenson very naturally wished him to have a profession to fall back upon should literature not prove a success, and it was agreed that he should read for the Bar. Louis, therefore, about the end of 1871, entered the office of the firm which is now known as Messrs Skene, Edwards, & Garson, W.S. The late Mr Skene, LL.D., was then senior partner of the firm. Another partner was the father of Mr J. R. P. Edwards, who has kindly supplied the following very interesting facts about Robert Louis Stevenson while he was undergoing his legal training in his office.

'Mr Stevenson entered the office, which was then in 18 Hill Street, in 1871, and left it about the middle of the year 1873, and was afterwards called to the Bar. His position in the office was neither that of a clerk nor of an apprentice, but merely of a person gaining some know-ledge of business. He never received any salary, and, as is usual with aspirants for the Bar, his position was in no way subject to the ordinary office discipline. After search-ing through papers which were written in the office during the time Stevenson was in the office, I find a good many papers which were written by him, but they are all merely copies of documents, and I can find no trace of any deeds which were actually drawn up by him. This is no doubt accounted for, firstly, because he was not experienced enough in the drafting of deeds, and, secondly, because he may have found the somewhat dry intricacies of con-

veyancing, which are for the most part governed by hard
and fast rules of law, foreign to his marvellous imagination.

'I have not been able to trace any of the staff of the
office who were in it with Robert Louis Stevenson, with
the exception of two men, who seem to remember little
about him, but they said that he was very reserved and
kept very much to himself. One of the men did not even
know that he was the great Stevenson. The other man,
however, said that he remembered that Stevenson had, as
he described it to me, "an awful notion of the Pentland
hills, and was that fond of talking about them." I believe
he was very fond of scribbling pieces of writing on odd
pieces of paper in his spare moments, but, unfortunately,
I can find no trace of these; but that is not to be
wondered at, as the firm have removed to two different
houses since Stevenson was in the office.

'Mr Skene, who was head partner of the firm during
the time that Stevenson was in the office, had always a
great admiration for his writings, and shortly before his
(Mr Skene's) death he said that it was a great regret to
him that he had not known him better, and recognised in
him a brother in letters. My father, who saw a good deal
more of Stevenson, says that he struck him as being a
very shy and nervous man, or rather, as he then was, a boy.
My father also states that Stevenson was a tremendous
walker, and that he used often to come into the office
in the morning in the somewhat unprofessional garb of
walking kit, having covered a good many miles before
breakfast.'

The office staff in 1871 consisted of ten men. Six of
them have died, two cannot now be traced, and the

remaining two mentioned by Mr Edwards are very old men.

Mr Edwards also says that in one deed which was written by Louis Stevenson there are five errors on two short pages, so that although the handwriting in it is neat, round, and clear, it is evident that his thoughts were not on his work, and that he was no more diligent in law than he had been in engineering. His handwriting, although neat and distinct, can hardly be called pretty, he seemed to use a good deal of ink in those days as the down strokes are all black and heavy. In spite of his lack of interest in his office work he passed advocate with credit on 14th July 1875, was called to the Bar on the 15th, and had his first brief on the 23rd.

He duly donned a wig and gown during the following session, and the delicate face that was so grave and refined looked very picturesque with the luminous eyes gleaming out from under the grey horse-hair. He joined the ranks of those 'Briefless Barristers' whose business it is to walk the hall of the Parliament House in search of clients. He had either one or two briefs, but he gave them away as he never acted as an advocate. His mother treasured the shillings he got for them among her relics of his early days.

Although his connection with the Parliament House was totally devoid of that professional success that ultimately leads to a seat on the Bench—but for which Mr Stevenson had no desire—it was not without its uses as an education for that other success by reason of which very many people who have never seen his face know and love him to-day. If his sojourn within those venerable halls was useless for law it was fruitful for literature, and one can imagine that as he now and then haunted the courts and listened to the advocates and the judges he was already, from a study of the Bench of the present, laying the foundation for those brilliant pictures of the judges of a ruder past which he gives us in Lord Preston-grange or Lord Hermiston. It is not very fair or very complimentary to the judges of 1875 to compare them with such a creation as Lord Hermiston, but it was not much more than half a century, before their day, that customs and manners like his were possible.

The robes, the forms, the etiquette, and the procedure of the Court of Session are still a sufficiently picturesque survival of an older time ; and to a mind like Mr Stevenson's that short association with the historic Parliament House, with its far-reaching traditions and with the acting majesty of the law in Scotland that is so old and so unchanged an institution, which to-day employs the very words and phrases of bygone centuries, and still holds, in many points, to the structure of the ancient Roman Law, could not fail to be interesting and useful. Like Sir Walter Scott, when he too walked in the Advocates' Hall, he no doubt found much that was worth studying in the old law procedure as well as in the men and manners of his own day, and appreciated to the full the magnificent library in its dark and silent rooms that are such a contrast to the bustle of the courts, and every corner of which is teeming with history.

But his heart was not in the Law Courts, and already in that book-lined study at 17 Heriot Row, the window of which looked over the Forth to Fife, and the walls of which were so temptingly covered with books, his real life-work had begun. No treat was greater, no honour more esteemed, than a visit to that study and a learned disquisition there on its owner's favourite books or methods of work.

Walking up and down with the hands thrown out in gesticulations, semi-foreign but eminently natural — for did not the child of three do it while repeating hymns on that walk to Broughton !—Mr Stevenson gave his opinions on matters grave and gay. Possibly he even produced his note-books, and with a slim finger between the leaves showed us the practice which he considered necessary for the creation of an author and the making of a style, breaking off in the middle of his disquisition to quote some master of the art or to take from the shelves a favourite book and read aloud a pertinent illustration of the subject in hand.

Boswell's *Life of Johnson*, Borrow's *Bible in Spain*, the Bible itself, Butler's *Hudibras*, George Meredith's novels, then less appreciated than now, were all books for a better knowledge of which some of us had to thank those visits to the study: on the shelves too were Bulwer Lytton, Sir Walter Scott, the old dramatists, ballads, and chapbooks, and innumerable favourites that had a place in his heart as well as in his bookcase.

Keen and clever were the criticisms he made on them —criticisms that come back to one with the pathos of ' a voice that is still ' when one reads in his *Gossip on Romance* and *A Humble Remonstrance* his delight in Boswell, his pleasure in *All Sorts and Conditions of Men,* and his admiration for Scott as a Prince of

Romance writers, for whose style he had not one good word to say!

He had early edited and written for amateur magazines, and when only sixteen he wrote a pamphlet on the Pentland Rising of 1666,* which is still in existence but a great rarity; the same subject inspired a romance, and another romance was composed about Hackston of Rathillet, that sombre and impressive witness of the murder of Archbishop Sharp, whose conscientious refusal either to take part for or against the victim had from childhood appealed to Mr Stevenson as pathetic and picturesque. He also wrote in those days a poetical play, some dramatic dialogues, and a pamphlet called *An Appeal to the Church of Scotland*, in which his father was keenly interested. The style in his early letters and notes of travel was excellent, but he destroyed most of his writings at that time as he worked for practice rather than for publication. He contributed frequently about 1871 to the *University Magazine*, in which, as he kindly lent it to us, some of us had the pleasure of reading *An Old Gardener* and *A Pastoral*, two papers of much promise, very full of outdoor life, the caller air of the Pentland hills and the scent of the old-fashioned flowers in the Swanston garden.

Edinburgh, as a picturesque, historic city, he loved with a life's devotion; Edinburgh, as a frivolous social centre, he despised; so some of the strictures he made on it in

* This is to be found reprinted in the Edinburgh Edition, in which are also published for the first time the *Amateur Emigrant* in full, a fragmentary romance, *The Great North Road*, and other papers and letters, &c., not hitherto known to the public.

Picturesque Edinburgh, published in 1879, and beautifully illustrated by Mr Sam Bough and Mr Lockhart, gave dire offence at the time to the denizens of ' Auld Reekie,' and are in some quarters hardly pardoned even now when death and fame have made Scotland's capital value her gifted son at his true worth.

In 1873 Mr Stevenson made the acquaintance of Mr Sidney Colvin and a life-long friendship ensued. The older man was of great use in many ways to the younger, whose genius he early discovered, and whose leaning to literature he encouraged. In the interesting preface to *The Vailima Letters* Mr Colvin tells of his help in that time of trial, and that he used his influence to persuade the parents that Louis had found his real vocation in literature, and ought to follow it. No doubt when the large and full *Life* of Mr Stevenson, which Mr Colvin is preparing, appears, he will have much of interest to tell of that turning-point in the young man's life. He was of service also in introducing his friend to editors, and Mr Stevenson's first serious appearance in literature was an essay on *Roads* sent by Mr Colvin to Mr Hamerton, the editor of *The Portfolio*, in 1873. It appeared shortly, and was followed by more work there and elsewhere; *Cornhill*, *Longmans*, and *Macmillan* having all before long printed papers by the new writer. In Macmillan the paper *Ordered South* appeared in April 1874, and had a pathetic interest as it was an account of the first of its author's many pilgrimages in search of health, which, after he grew to manhood, were to make up so much of his life's experience.

In *Fraser's*, *Scribner's*, *The New Amphion*, *The*

Magazine of Art, his early work also found acceptance,
and he occasionally contributed to *The Contemporary
Review* and *The English Illustrated,* a list of well-
known magazines in the home country which makes the
more remarkable the refusal of the American papers to
use his contributions largely, during his stay in San Francisco and Monterey.

Of that charming dreamy sketch of those days, *Will o'
the Mill,* which appeared in *Cornhill,* Mr Hamerton
wrote in the highest terms of praise.   Most of these early
essays, sketches, and tales have been republished, and in
the beautiful *Edinburgh Edition* of his works, presently
being seen through the press by Mr Colvin and Mr
Baxter, and all but completed, his many admirers will
be able to read all that came from his busy and graceful
pen.

In 1878 Mr Stevenson's first book, *An Inland Voyage,*
was published by Messrs Chatto & Windus.   It is a
bright, fresh account of a trip in canoes, ' The Arethusa '
and ' The Cigarette,' made by Mr Stevenson and his friend
the late Sir Walter G. Simpson up the Oise and the
Sambre.   The travellers had unique opportunities of
observing people and scenery, and of these the writer
made the most, consequently the book is full of pretty
pictures of scenery and quaint touches of human life
which make it charming reading.

' There is nothing,' he says, ' so quiet and so much
alive as a woodland.   And surely of all smells in the
world the smell of many trees is sweetest and most
satisfying.'

These are the reflections of a man to whom the teem-

ing silence of the woods was very dear, and who, in
Prince Otto, afterwards wrote a prose poem on the
mystery of the woods which Thoreau himself could
not have excelled.

'If we were charged so much a head for sunsets, or if
God sent round a drum before the hawthorns came into
flower, what a work we should make about their beauty.
But these things, like good companions, stupid people
early cease to observe;' a state of affairs fortunately
incomprehensible to Mr Stevenson, who had not only a
keen perception of the beauty of the world but 'that
inward eye which is the bliss of solitude' that enabled
him to recall and reproduce from memory these pleasures
of the past.

The volume which ends with the statement that 'The
most beautiful adventures are not those we go to seek,' is
from its first page to its last brightly readable and full of
pleasant and graceful thoughts and fancies. Its style is
more mannered and less excellent than that of his later
work, but it already appealed to that cultured public who
welcomed the appearance of a new writer likely to make
his mark as a 'maker' of English style.

In 1895 *An Inland Voyage* had run into its seventh
edition; it was followed by the even more popular *Travels
in the Cevennes with a Donkey*, which the same publishers
sent out in 1879, and which in 1895 had reached a ninth
edition.

On this occasion Mr Stevenson travelled alone. He
had been living for a time in the little town of Le
Monastier, fifteen miles from Le Puy, and here, in the
late autumn, he bought an ass which he called 'Modes-

tine,' and with it, to the great interest of his simple
neighbours, started on a tour in the Cevennes. The
pair set forth speeded on their way by many good wishes
and, in spite of a slow pace and not a few misfortunes
with the baggage and the pack-saddle, the tour was most
successful. As to Modestine's pace her master describes
it as being 'as much slower than a walk as a walk is
slower than a run'!

The experiences of the traveller in the crisp, bright
autumn weather and the perfect scenery of the Cevennes
were thoroughly enjoyable. The simple peasantry and the
homely innkeepers proved more friendly and agreeable
than those along the route of the canoeists had done.
In the monastery of 'Our Lady of the Snows' he
had a kindly welcome from the Trappist monks, who
seemed to have found it possible to break their stern
rule of silence in their eagerness to convert him to
Roman Catholicism. Among themselves this rule of
silence and the poorest diet is rigidly enforced, and as
the traveller left their hospitable doors he 'blessed God
that he was free to wander, free to hope, and free to
love.'

In the country of the Camisards—that little sect of
persecuted religionists whose fierce brief struggle against
the tyranny of the Church of Rome he so graphically
describes—the descendant of Scotch Covenanters found
himself at home, and at 'Pont de Montvert' his heart
beat in a certain stern sympathy with the persecuted
remnant, who here slew Du Chayla, and with that strange
weird prophet Spirit Séguir, who, after the deed was
done, and he was about to suffer death for it at the

stake, said : 'My soul is like a garden full of shelter and fountains.'

The rising took place on 24th July 1702, and Mr Stevenson says of it :

' 'Tis a wild night's work with its accompaniment of psalms ; and it seems as if a psalm must always have a sound of threatening in that town upon the Tarn.'

There is a delightful description of a night among the firs in which the very spirit of nature breathes through his words, and his reason for travelling as he does is happy and convincing.

' I travel for travel's sake.   The great affair is to move, to feel the needs and hitches of our life more nearly ; to come down off the feather bed of civilisation and find the globe granite under foot and stern with cutting flints. Alas ! as we get up in life and are more pre-occupied with our affairs, even a holiday is a thing to be worked for.'

Many people have all through life a closer acquaintance with ' the globe granite under foot' than with ' the feather bed of civilisation,' and daily bread even more than a holiday is a thing to be worked for.   But Mr Stevenson's lines had hitherto fallen in very pleasant places, and he had not as yet entered as seriously as he had to do later into the bitter battle of life.

After twelve days together he sold Modestine at St Jean du Gard and made his return journey by diligence. This book, like the first, was widely read and heartily appreciated as soon as it appeared.

CHAPTER VII

WANDERINGS IN SEARCH OF HEALTH

'Know how sublime a thing it is
To suffer and be strong.'—LONGFELLOW.

MR STEVENSON's health, although always a cause of more or less anxiety, was from time to time somewhat better; else he could hardly have taken such very active holidays as are recorded in *An Inland Voyage*, and the tour *Through the Cevennes with a Donkey*. Nevertheless the delicacy was there, and it not only increased in 1873 but culminated in the autumn of that year in the first of those serious attacks of illness which afterwards frequently caused himself so much suffering and his friends such keen distress all through the life that, in spite of them, he lived so bravely.

In the October of 1873 the doctors took so grave a view of his indisposition that they ordered him south for the winter, and on the 5th of November he started on the first of those pilgrimages in search of health of which he says, somewhat sadly, in writing of his grandfather, in his paper on *The Old Manse :*

'He sought health in his youth in the Isle of Wight;

I have sought it in both hemispheres, but whereas he found it and kept it, I am still on the quest.'

The anxiety and distress of his parents during that winter were naturally intense, and there is something tragic in the dates so carefully preserved:

'Lou started on 5th November 1873.'

'He returned to Heriot Row on 26th April 1874.'

Ordered South appeared in *Macmillan* for that same April, and in its very beauty there is a most painful pathos. The polish of its style, its exquisitely chosen words, give to it something of the sadness of the brilliant autumn tints on a wood, the red gold and the glory of decay. It is a brave paper and it is an intensely sad one, the sadness in which goes straight to the reader's heart, while the courage takes his respect by storm. No wonder it calls forth universal sympathy; too many homes have been darkened by the dread sentence 'Ordered South,' too many sufferers have obeyed it in life's gay noonday, or in its sunny prime, and few, alas! very few, have even returned to face the long struggle with fate that Mr Stevenson fought so heroically! This was the first, for him, of many journeys 'South'; for although the winter in the Riviera sent him back somewhat stronger, the inherent delicacy was still there, and time after time, in the twenty years and eleven months that he lived after the November morning when he set out on that melancholy journey, the recurrence of the graver symptoms of his malady obliged him to seek sunnier skies and warmer climates.

Scotland which he loved, the grey skies, the greyer mists, the snell winds,—that even in his happy Samoan life his exile's heart hungered for to the last,—were fatal to his delicate lungs, and year by year he was compelled to live less and less in his old Edinburgh home.

In 1880 when he brought his wife to Scotland to visit his parents his health was so precarious that he had to hurry abroad before the winter, and he and his wife and stepson went to Davos where they met and formed a pleasant friendship with Mr J. A. Symonds and his family. On their return it was hoped that the climate of the south of England might suit Mr Stevenson and be conveniently near London for literary business and literary friendships, so he and his wife and son settled at Bournemouth in a house called Skerryvore, after the famous lighthouse so dear to all the Stevensons. Here too, alas ! his enemy found him out ; and chronic, indifferent health, with not infrequent attacks of lung disease in its more serious forms, finally obliged him about 1887 to take another journey to America in the hope that it might do him good.

Through all his life the shadow of death was never quite out of sight for him or for those who loved him ; the skeleton hand was continually beckoning to him. When we think what that means, in a man's life, we realise with amazement his charming cheerfulness, his wonderful courage, and the magnitude of his work, the exactitude of his methods, the carefulness of his research, appeal to us as something positively heroic in one so handicapped by adverse fate.

When many men in despair would have given in he fought on ; and the sum of his work, the length of his years—comparatively short as these were—witness to the truth that *will* can do many things. He willed to fight,

he willed to live, he scorned to drop by the wayside, or
to die one day before the battle was hopeless, and he
fought his fight with a smiling face and a gay courage
that was as fine a thing in its way as an act which has
won a Victoria Cross; nay, finer, perhaps, for the struggle
was not of minutes, or of hours, but of a lifetime, a stern
prolonged tussle with death, in which he was never
selfish, never peevish, always thoughtful of others, invariably merry and bright, with a wonderful sparkling
whimsical mirth that had in it no touch of bitterness
or of cynicism. Even the last years of life, when the
need to work hard for an income that would sufficiently
maintain his household, made brain work, under conditions of physical weakness, often peculiarly trying, were
largely full of the same marvellous pluck and illumined
by the same sunny temperament.

In the years between 1873 and 1879, in the summer
of which he went to San Francisco, he had sought health
in many places with a varying degree of success. He
had seen much of life and, as he was an excellent
linguist, had everywhere formed friendships with men of
all nationalities, and was thus enabled to study at his
leisure continental life and manners. He frequently
stayed at Fontainbleau, where he had a Stevenson cousin
studying art, and the pleasant unconventional life of
the student settlement at Brabazon was very attractive
to a man of Mr Stevenson's temperament. His first visit
to the artist colony was paid in 1875, and it was often
repeated.

His wanderings had unfortunately brought no permanent improvement to his health so, for that and other

reasons, it occurred to him in 1879 to go to San Francisco to see if the Californian climate would be of benefit
to him.   Eager as ever to study life in all its phases
and from every point of view he took his passage in an
emigrant ship—where he tells us he posed as a mason
and played his part but indifferently well!—and at New
York resolved to continue his journey across America
by emigrant train.

In the graphic account of his experiences, in the
volume of essays entitled *Across the Plains*, and in *The
Amateur Emigrant*, he describes what must have been
a very trying time to a man of his refined upbringing and
frail constitution.   But he looks, here as elsewhere, at
the bright side of people and things; and even for the
Chinaman, from whom the other emigrants hold themselves aloof, he has a good word to say.   He keenly
observed everything from his fellow-passengers, the character of the newsboys on the cars, and the petty oppres-
sions of the railway officials to the glories of the scenery
on that marvellous journey of which Joaquin Miller says:—

> ' We glide through golden seas of grain,
>   We shoot, a shining comet, through
>   The mountain range, against the blue,
>   And then, below the walls of snow,
>   We blow the desert dust amain,
>   We see the orange groves below,
>   We rest beneath the oaks, and we
>   Have cleft a continent in twain.'

After the long rush across the plains, Mr Stevenson's
heart bounded with joy when he caught a glimpse of
'a huge pine-forested ravine, a foaming river, and a sky
already coloured with the fires of dawn.'

'You will scarce believe it,' he says, 'how my heart leaped at this. It was like meeting one's wife. I had come home again—home from unsightly deserts to the green and habitable corners of the earth.'

By the afternoon they had reached Sacramento, which he writes of as 'a city of gardens in a plain of corn,' and before the dawn of the next day the train was drawn up at the Oaklands side of San Francisco Bay. The day broke as they crossed the ferry, and he says :

'The fog was rising over the citied hills of San Francisco; the bay was perfect, not a ripple, scarce a stain upon its blue expanse, everything was waiting breathless for the sun.

'A spot of gold first lit upon the head of Talampais and then widened downwards on its shapely shoulder ' . . . and by-and-bye

'The tall hills Titan discovered,'

'and the city of San Francisco and the bay of gold and corn were lit from end to end with summer daylight.'

In *The Old Pacific Capital* he writes delightfully of San Francisco and the surge of its 'toss'd and tumbled sea,' that echoes forever around Monterey and its woods of oaks and pines and cedars. He has much that is interesting to tell of the curious contrast between San Francisco, modern and American, and Monterey, the 'Old Pacific Capital,' so full of a pathetic and a half-forgotten history. He has a deep sympathy with its refined and impoverished Spanish gentle-folk and their unpractical ideas of what is honourable ; and he predicts that the people who do not consider it etiquette to look through an important paper before signing it are, in spite of America's assertions that they are well able to take care of themselves, little likely to survive long in a world of Yankee sharpness and smartness.

He revelled in the beautiful woods so often devastated by forest fires. On one occasion, he says, he came perilously near lynching, for he applied a match to the dry moss which clings to the bark of the trees to see if it were so peculiarly ignitable as to be an important factor in the rapid spread of a fire. In a moment flames broke out all over the tree, and he found to his horror that he had started a fresh fire of his own very difficult to put out, and exceedingly likely to arouse the indignation of the men who were struggling to beat out the existing conflagration, to the point of lynching the too officious stranger.

The solemn boom of the Pacific was a constant delight to him, and he gloried in the ever-changing lights and shadows on the sea. If he did not attain to permanent good health while at San Francisco and Monterey he at least found there something else which made for the lasting happiness of his life, as it was there that he married his wife.

After spending about seven years of married life at Bournemouth he again, in 1887, tried a visit to America. His health, however, did not improve, and, during the winter of 1887 and 1888, when he was at Saranac Lake, he speaks of himself, in *The Vailima Letters*, as having been—in the graphic Scots words—'far through'; and the idea occurred to him of chartering a yacht and going for a voyage in the South Seas. His mother on this occasion accompanied the family party, and between 1888 and 1890 they sailed about among the lovely islands of the South Sea, visiting Honolulu, and finally touching at Apia in Samoa, where they promptly fell in love with the beauty of the scenery and the charm of the climate.

On this voyage, as always, Mr Stevenson made friends wherever he went, and had much pleasant intercourse with wandering Europeans, missionaries and natives.

On her return to Edinburgh, after this cruise with him, his mother used to give most entertaining accounts of the feasts given in their honour by the native chiefs, and of the quaint gifts bestowed on them. At an afternoon tea-party at 17 Heriot Row, shortly before the home there was finally broken up, she put on for our benefit the wreath—still wonderfully green—that had been given to her to wear at one of those island festivities. She had promised the sable majesty who gave it to her to be photographed with it on, and to send him one of the copies. One of these photographs is beside me now, and is an excellent likeness. Close to it is the graceful one of her son, taken at Bournemouth, wearing his hair long, and one of the velvet coats that he loved, and it is a most curious contrast to the sturdy Scotsman, his father, who looks out at it from his frame, in conventional broadcloth and with the earnest gravity so characteristic of his face in repose.

Innumerable photographs, pictures, and busts, were taken of Robert Louis Stevenson, but not one of them has ever been a very real or a very satisfying likeness. In recent years one rarely sees an Academy Exhibition without one or more representations of the mobile face, the expression of which has, alas! eluded the grasp of even the best of artists.

The Stevenson party had been so charmed with Samoa, that, as the climate suited Louis admirably, they resolved to give up the Bournemouth home, buy some ground in Samoa, and finally settle there. So sometime about 1890 Vailima was bought, and building and reclaiming operations were begun, and, save for occasional visits to Sydney or Honolulu, Mr Stevenson and his household gave up personal communication with the busy and civilised world, and happily settled themselves in a peaceful life among the palms and the sunshine of the tropics and the friendly Samoan natives, who grew to be so deeply attached to them, and so proud of 'Tusitala.'

CHAPTER VIII

HIS MARRIAGE AND FRIENDSHIPS

> . . . ' What we seek is but our other self
> Other and higher, neither wholly like
> Nor wholly different, the half life the gods
> Retained when half was given—one the man
> And one the woman.' . . .—*Epic of Hades.*
>   L. MORRIS.

> ' Old friends are best, old coats that fit.'
>   —ROBERT RICHARDSON.

IT was naturally to be supposed that a man of Mr Stevenson's temperament, before whose eyes from his earliest childhood there had been present a woman good enough to give him the very highest ideal of womanhood, would not easily or lightly give his heart away. He knew that he longed for the best, and to nothing less than the best could he give his soul's worship. That he did not find his ideal in the beaten track of everyday social life, or among the gay and agreeable girls whom he met in his young manhood, is not surprising.

The element of romance, as well as the longing for what was noblest in womanhood, was in him; and romance for him was not embodied in a pretty young woman in a ball gown. Possibly he considered that the amusing advice as to matrimony which he gives in

Virginibus Puerisque, was as applicable to a man as to a woman, and that 'the bright' girl of Society was as apt to be a wearisome and an exacting helpmate as her brother, 'the bright boy of fiction,' against whom as a husband his essay warns the woman in search of marriage to whom he recommends, as a more comfortable partner, the man old enough to have loved before, and to have undergone something of an apprenticeship in devotion. Very pertinent also is his advice to men in the same essay, that kindred tastes are more likely to ensure lasting happiness than a fair face or an acceptable dowry.

Beneath the easy brightness of thought and style that make the essay so amusing and so readable, one sees that its writer knows his world well, and has given graver thought to matters matrimonial than at a first reading one is inclined to believe.

Holding firmly the faith that 'all things come to him who knows how to wait,' Mr Stevenson was in no hurry to realise his ideal, and it was not until he was between twenty-seven and thirty that he met the woman whom he chose for his wife. That there was an element of romance in their acquaintance altogether removed from everyday love stories made it all the more fitting an ending to that watchful waiting for what fate had to give him.

When Mr Stevenson arrived in San Francisco in 1879, there was living with her sister, at Monterey, Mrs Fanny Van de Grift Osbourne of Indiana. Mrs Osbourne had been married when very young, and her domestic experience was so unhappy that she had to obtain a divorce from her husband. She had, with her son and daughter, lived for some time in that student colony at Fontainbleau which Mr Stevenson knew and loved so well, and in after years they must have had in common many pleasant memories of people and places dear to both, so that his ideal of matrimony described in *Virginibus Puerisque* was realised, and he and his wife had 'many an old joke between them which time cannot wither nor custom stale.'

At a party, when in France, Mr Stevenson had much admired Mrs Osbourne and her daughter Belle, who married a Mr Strong, and who afterwards, in the Vailima days, became her step-father's secretary. The young girl he found very fresh and sweet with the gay brightness of youth, but of her mother his impression was much deeper, and he always spoke and wrote of her as the most beautiful and the most charming woman whom he had ever seen. Although she was several years his senior she was then in the very prime of a womanly beauty which, to judge from the photographs taken at Vailima more than ten years later, was only at its ripest when other women are beginning to think of growing old. No one who had even once looked into her dark eyes could fail to endorse Mr Stevenson's verdict, to realise her charm of person, or doubt for a moment the loveliness of nature and the nobility of soul to which these strange deep eyes were the index. She was indeed charming, and it was no wonder that such a nature as Mr Stevenson's found in her that 'other half' of the old Platonic tradition, the fortunate finding of which can alone make a marriage perfect.

The romantic and the unusual in the story comes in when, at the request of his doctor, Mrs Osbourne gave

willingly of her kindness and her skill in nursing to the
young man who was lying at point of death alone in a
far land. The child of the people with whom he was
boarding had been very ill, and when other folk left the
house of sickness, Mr Stevenson, who had liked his little
playfellow, remained to help the parents with the nursing,
and wore himself out in their service as only a man of
his rare human sympathy and tenderness of heart would
have done. The child recovered, and long years afterwards when the monument to his memory was erected
at San Francisco, the mother laid a wreath at its base in
remembrance of that unforgotten kindness. Unfortunately,
already far from well and suffering much from the effects
of the journey by emigrant ship and train and the stern
experience of 'roughing it' which that had entailed, Mr
Stevenson was quite unfit for the fatigue of nursing and
he became so ill that the doctor despaired of his life.
This doctor, who then and afterwards proved a very real
friend, was greatly distressed about his patient, especially
as the danger of his illness was greatly increased by the
lack of that skilled nursing which was there very difficult
to obtain. In such a case the physician could do much,
but a good nurse could do far more, so the doctor, in
his anxiety, recollected that Mrs Osbourne was, like himself, interested in the talented young Scotsman, and was
also possessed of a rare and womanly gift of nursing, and
he begged her to do what she could for his patient. She
responded to his appeal, and with her sister showed the
invalid a kindness so great that it did more to help his
recovery than the best of drugs could have done. He
was restored to a certain measure of health, and it may

thus be said that he owed his life to his future wife, but
he owed her much more for her unselfish devotion in his
time of weakness and loneliness, as a stranger in a strange
land, glorified to him all womanhood in her person, and
the man who knew what it was to have an ideal mother
was so peculiarly fortunate as to find an ideal wife also.
Two such natures as theirs were inevitably attracted to
each other, and it is not surprising that their friendship
deepened into love, or that in later years he says of her :

> ‘ Teacher, tender comrade, wife,
> A fellow-farer true through life,
> Heart-whole and soul-free,
> The august Father
> Gave to me.’

At San Francisco, on the 19th of May 1880, Robert
Louis Stevenson and Fanny Van de Grift Osbourne were
married, and there began for them that perfect life together which anxiety and illness could not cloud, and
which found its earthly termination when in that awful
and sudden moment in December 1894 Mr Stevenson
entered into ‘ the Rest Eternal.’

Belle Osbourne became Mrs Strong, and by-and-bye
she and her little boy Austin joined the Stevensons in
their home life. ‘ Sam,’ as Mr Lloyd Osbourne was
called in those days, accompanied them to England
when they made their home at Bournemouth. He was
a bright, eager boy when he used to appear in Edinburgh,
and one who was very welcome to the elder Stevensons
at Heriot Row. By-and-bye he went to the Edinburgh
University and there he was full of life and interest, keen
on pleasures, keen on friendships, interested in classes,

and even then there was something of the same earnestness, the same humour and brightness in him that characterised his stepfather and which made him, by-and-bye, with no small measure of the same gifts, his collaborater and friend. A friendship that was begun in very early days when the two told each other stories and issued romances from a toy printing-press, and when the junior received that delightful dedication of *Treasure Island* in which he is described as 'a young American gentleman' to whose taste the tale appeals.

Shortly after their marriage Mr and Mrs R. L. Stevenson had had the quaint experience of housekeeping so charmingly described in *Silverado Squatters*, but their first real home was at Skerryvore, and Bournemouth was the headquarters of the household until the necessities of Mr Stevenson's health again made them wanderers; and that move in 1887 finally ended in the purchase of Vailima, and the pitching of their camp in far Samoa.

The curtest mention of their Bournemouth life would be incomplete without some notice of the many friends who found it so easy to reach from London and so pleasant to visit, and who, themselves well known in the literary world, so greatly appreciated the genius of Mr Stevenson. Among old Edinburgh friends of long standing were his many Balfour and Stevenson cousins and his old comrades of early days, and among the latter Mr Charles Baxter and the late Sir Walter G. Simpson held a principal place in his regard. Mr Sidney Colvin he had first met in 1873, Mr Henley he first knew in Edinburgh about the end of 1874, and Mr Edmund Gosse was another much valued friend of long standing.

Mr Colvin was to the last one of the friends highest in his regard, and to him were written *The Vailima Letters.*

His wonderful attire, at the Savile Club and elsewhere in orthodox London, at first astonished and somewhat repelled literary men accustomed to a more conventional garb than the velvet coats, the long loose hair, and the marvellous ties Mr Stevenson delighted in; but very soon they found out the charm of the personality that lay behind a certain eccentricity of appearance, and Mr Leslie Stephen, Mr James Payn, Dr Appleton, Professor Clifford, Mr Cosmo Monkhouse, and Mr George Meredith, whom he met in 1878 and whose work he so much admired, were numbered among his life-long friends. Mr Henley's description of him in these days is better than any picture:

> ' Thin-legged, thin-chested, slight unspeakably,
> Neat-footed, weak-fingered, in his face,—
> Lean, large-boned, curved of beak, and touched with race,
> Bold-lipped, rich tinted, mutable as the sea,
> The brown eyes radiant with vivacity,—
> There shines a brilliant and romantic grace,
> A spirit intense and rare, with trace on trace
> Of passion, impudence, and energy.'

Another friend of those days, Mr Andrew Lang, also lets his friendship run into rhyme, and sends across the seas to the author of *The Master of Ballantrae* a quaint greeting in the best of Southland Doric:

> ' Whan Suthern winds gar spindrift flee
> Abune the clachan, faddumes hie,
> Whan for the cluds I canna see
> The bonny lift,
> I'd fain indite an odd to thee
> Had I the gift ! . . .

. . . ' O Louis, you that writes in Scots,
Ye're far awa' frae stirks and stots,
Wi' drookit herdies, tails in knots,
    An unco way !
My mirth's like thorns aneth the pots
    In Ballantrae ! '

To this Mr Stevenson promptly replied in equally fine
Doric, and with a playful allusion to the early ' brindled '
hair which gives to Mr Andrew Lang an appearance
venerable beyond his years.

Mr Crockett, in the delightful dedication to *The Stickit
Minister*, celebrates his friendship with Mr Stevenson;
and among the younger school of writers, for whose work
he had so generous an appreciation, he had many friends
as well as admirers.   Mr Barrie, Mr Rudyard Kipling, Mr
Le Galliene, and a host of others loved him as a friend, as
well as looked up to him as a literary leader.   To many
of them he wrote charming letters, although in several
cases no actual meeting had ever taken place.   It was
a keen disappointment to both men that circumstances
prevented Mr Rudyard Kipling from paying a visit to
Samoa.

In his island home he was not forgetful of his ' own
romantic town,' nor of the interests of one, at least, of its
publishing firms, whose travellers and agents he intro-
duced to new fields of usefulness in India and the South
Seas.   One of his own favourite books was *Coral Island*, by
Mr R. M. Ballantyne, published by the Messrs Nelson.

But Stevenson, whose charm of personality was even
greater than his fame, had other friends, whose friendship
is not measured by the intellect but by the heart.   Little
children and young folk everywhere loved the man whose

Child's Garden of Verses shows such a marvellous insight into the hearts of children.

The ass Modestine, the Samoan horse Jack, well knew that the indignant flow of language meant nothing, and that their master's heart was altogether in the right place, although, when they were too provoking, his words might be very unparliamentary.

For dogs he had as great an attraction as they had for him, and the master of Coolin the wise, and Woggs, or Bogue, the gallant, discourses as few men could do about canine thoughts and feelings in his essay *The Character of Dogs.*

No fear of his being among the foolish people who remark that 'they like dogs in their proper place,' and, as he stingingly adds, say, ' " Poo' fellow ! Poo' fellow ! " and are themselves far poorer ! ' He knew, because he had taken the trouble to study him, that 'to the dog of gentlemanly feelings, theft and falsehood are disgraceful vices.'

CHAPTER IX

HIS ESSAYS AND POEMS

'Golden thoughts that ever will resound,
And be re-echoed to the utmost parts of land and sea.'
—R. S. Mutch.

Mr Stevenson inherited both from the Stevenson and
Balfour families some measure of literary talent. His
father and his grandfather had written with considerable
acceptance on the subject of their profession. His father
also wrote on religious matters, and at least one of these
pamphlets was believed to be of lasting value by competent judges. On scientific and engineering subjects
his work was thought so excellent, and was so well known,
that R. L. Stevenson tells, with some amusement, that he
was surprised to find in the New World it was his father
and not himself who was considered the important author.
The Life of Robert Stevenson, of Bell Rock fame, written
by David Stevenson, is a very interesting book.

Among his mother's relatives the gift of fluent and
graceful expression is also widely diffused, and in common
with Mrs Thomas Stevenson and her son, not a few of the
Balfour connection have been very charming letter writers,
in the days when letters were worth receiving, and not the
hurried and uncharacteristic scraps which do duty for
present-day correspondence.

He himself considered that he inherited his literary talent largely from his father's family, but there is interesting proof that even in his grandfather's day it was inherent also in his Balfour ancestors. The minister of Colinton wrote verses in his youth, and a sonnet preserved by his surviving son and daughter is interesting as a proof of his earnest mind and his literary skill. It was written on the fly-leaf of a folio copy of *Pearson on the Creed*, presented to him by his friend, the Reverend Patrick Macfarlane, who became, about 1832, minister of the West Church at Greenock, and is dated 18th May 1801.

> ' My friend, my Patrick, let me boast the name,
> For my breast glows with no inferior flame,
> This gift was thine, expressive of thy love,
> Which spurning earthborn joys for those above
> Would teach my friend in sacred lore to grow,
> And feel the truths impressive as they flow.
> While with our faith our kindred bosoms glow,
> And love to God directs our life below,
> One view of things now seen, and things to come,
> But pilgrims here, a future state our home,
> Nor time, nor death, our friendship shall impair,
> Begun below, but rendered perfect there.'

More than one of the old gentleman's family inherited his talent for graceful and forcible writing. His son, Dr George W. Balfour, has written two well-known medical books which have brought to him a large measure of fame. These are *Clinical Lectures on Diseases of the Heart*, and the even more popular *The Senile Heart*. About the latter he tells an excellent story. A well-known literary critic, seeing the book lying on the table, thought

it a work of fiction with an admirable and unique title,
carried it off for review, and found to his disgust it was a
learned medical treatise.   Dr John Balfour, an elder son
of the manse, wrote papers in *The Indian Annals* and
The Edinburgh Medical Journal, which were very highly
esteemed.

In the younger generation, a cousin of Mr R. L.
Stevenson, Mrs Beckwith Sitwell, has written much and
pleasantly, principally for young people.   Another cousin,
Mrs Marie Clothilde Balfour, has already gained for herself no inconsiderable repute as a novelist, her third book,
The Fall of the Sparrow, having been considered by
competent critics one of the notable books of last year.
Her father was a son of the Colinton manse, who died
young, and she is married to her cousin—Dr G. W.
Balfour's son — who can also, like his father, write
acceptably on medical and other subjects.

It is not surprising, therefore, that the bent towards
literature which appears in both families should in Robert
Louis Stevenson have been developed into that rare gift
which men call genius.   While he was still a careless
student of twenty, his papers in *The Edinburgh University
Magazine* possessed a peculiar attraction, and appealed to
cultured minds with a charm not often found in the work
of so young a writer.

An Old Gardener and *A Pastoral* especially had much
of the depth of thought and the finish of style which so
largely characterised Mr Stevenson's later work.   Interesting and delightful as he is as a story-teller, there is in
his essays a graceful fascination which makes them for
many of his readers infinitely more satisfying than the

most brilliant of his tales. In the essays you seem to
meet the man face to face, to listen to his spoken thoughts,
to see the grave and the gay reflections of his mind, to
enjoy with him ' the feast of reason and the flow of soul '
provided by the writers into whose company he takes you,
or to return with him to his boyhood, and, in *The Old
Manse* and *Random Memories* see familiar places and
people touched by the light of genius, and made as
wonderful to your own commonplace understanding as to
the intense and high-souled boy who wandered about
among them, hearing and seeing the everyday things of
life as only the romancist and the poet can hear and see
them.

His style, too—strong and virile as it is in his tales—
attains, one almost fancies, its full perfection in his essays.
The thoughts, both grave and gay, are presented in a
dainty dress that is peculiarly fitted to do them justice.
There is room in this quiet writing, disturbed by no
exigencies of plot, to give perfect scope to the grace and
the leisure which are the great charms of Mr Stevenson's
work. One can take up a volume of the essays or a
slim book of verses at any time and dip into it as one
would into some clear and cold mountain well, full of
refreshment for the weary wayfarer, and, like the well,
it is sure to give one an invigorating sense of keen
enjoyment, to take one far from the dusty highways of
life and plunge one into the depth and coolness of the
wide silence of nature, or to fill one's mind with strong
and worthy thoughts gleaned from the world of men and
books.

In his *Familiar Studies of Men and Books*, published,

in one volume, by Messrs Chatto & Windus in 1882, with a charming dedication to his father, Mr Stevenson gives in the preface a most interesting account of his own fuller point of view regarding the studies which had originally appeared in the *New Quarterly*, *Macmillan*, and *Cornhill*. The essays deal with such well-known men as Knox, Burns, Thoreau, Charles of Orleans, Samuel Pepys, and others, and are always fresh and agreeable reading. The papers on Knox and Burns have an especial interest for Mr Stevenson's fellow-countrymen who naturally appreciate the judgment of a later day genius on the character and work of the two men who have had so wide an influence on Scottish life and feeling.

To John Knox Scotland largely owes her reformed religion, her rigid presbyterianism, and it is, to many people, a new and an interesting phase of the character of the great Reformer—who so enjoyed brow-beating Queen Mary—that Mr Stevenson shows, when he depicts Knox as the confidential friend of the religious women of his day, writing letters to them, comforting them in domestic trials, even shedding tears with them, and keeping up, through a harassed and busy life, these friendships which seem to have been as great a source of pleasure to the Reformer as to the ladies.

Of Robert Burns, the peasant poet, whose songs did as much to bring back the sunshine into everyday Scotch life as the Reformer's homilies did to banish it, Mr Stevenson writes with sympathy and tenderness. For the work he is full of admiration ; for the man, whose circumstances and temperament made his whole life a difficult walking in slippery places where the best of men could hardly have refrained from falling, he has a gentle understanding, a manly pity. There was much in the poet's life and temperament repellent to a nature like Mr Stevenson's, but there was far more where the human feeling of man to man and of soul to soul could touch with comprehension, so that in his paper, and more especially in his preface, we find him giving to Scotland's national bard an ungrudging admiration in his struggles after the right, and no petty condemnation when he lapsed and fell from his own higher ideals.

Of Walt Whitman and Thoreau, both most interesting studies in the volume, he has much that is stimulating to say ; and many readers, who may not have time or opportunity for deep personal research, will find his essays on *Villon, Victor Hugo's Romances, Samuel Pepys, Yoshida Torajiro* and *Charles of Orleans* a very pleasant means of obtaining a great deal of information in a very limited space.

In the early essays, republished in volume form in 1881 by Messrs Chatto & Windus, under the title *Virginibus Puerisque*, Mr Stevenson discourses delightfully on many things, touching, for instance, with a light hand but a wise heart on matrimony and love-making, and the little things, so small in themselves, so large as they bulk for happiness or misery, that go to make peace or discord in married life. It is all done with a pointed pen and a smiling face; but its lightness covers wisdom, and it is full of sound counsel and makes wiser reading for young men and maidens than many books of more apparent gravity.

That pathos always lay close behind his playful mockeries and was never far away from the man whose paper on *Ordered South* is like the bravely repressed cry of all his fellow-sufferers the companion paper on *El Dorado* proves convincingly.   Under its graceful phrases there lies deep and strong sympathy for toil, for hope deferred and longed for, for the disappointment of attainment, for the labour that after all has so often to be its own reward.

Between 1880 and 1885 Mr Stevenson collaborated with Mr Henley in the writing of four plays which were privately printed, *Deacon Brodie* in 1880, *Beau Austin* in 1884, *Admiral Guinea* in 1884, and *Robert Macaire* in 1885—the whole being finally published in volume form in an edition limited to 250 copies, in 1896. *Beau Austin* was acted in 1890 at The Haymarket, and quite recently *Admiral Guinea* has been played with Mr Sydney Valentine in the part of David Pew, but in spite of the literary distinction of the collaborators the plays have not been a great success on the stage.

In the later papers, ' A Christmas Sermon,' ' A Letter to a Young Gentleman,' and ' Pulvis et Umbra,' in the volume of collected essays called *Across the Plains,* the note of pathos which appears now and then in *Virginibus Puerisque* is even more forcibly struck.   The writer is older, he has known more of life and of suffering, he has more than once looked death closely in the face, and, though his splendid courage is there all the time, the sadness of humanity is more apparent than in most of his work. The other essays in this volume are very pleasant reading, and *Across the Plains* and *The Old and New Pacific Capitals* give most graphic descriptions of the life and scenery on the shore of the Pacific, and of the journey to get there.

In 'Random Memories' in the same volume, he goes back to his boyhood, and we meet him at home beside the 'Scottish Sea,' under grey Edinburgh skies, larking with his fellow-boys in their autumn holidays, touring with his father in *The Pharos* round the coast of Fife, and later gaining some knowledge of harbour construction at Anstruther, and on the bleak shores of Caithness, an unwilling student of engineering, for whom, apart from the open air and the romance of a harbour or a light tower, his profession had no charms.

Not the least pleasant of his volumes of *Essays* is that called *Memories and Portraits*, published by Messrs Chatto & Windus in 1887, and dedicated to his mother, whom his father's death in the May of that year had so recently made a widow. In it there is a most interesting paper entitled 'Thomas Stevenson,' in which he writes very appreciatively of that father who was so great a man in the profession which the son admired although he could not follow it. Here, too, are papers on 'The Manse,' that old home of his grandfather at Colinton which he when a child loved so well; on the old gardener at Swanston, who so lovingly tended the vegetables of which he remarked to his mistress, when told to send in something choice for the pot, that 'it was mair blessed to give than to receive,' but gave her

of his best all the same, and who loved the old-fashioned
flowers, and gave a place to

> ' Gardener's garters, shepherd's purse,
> Batchelors' buttons, lady's smock,
> And the Lady Hollyhock.'

In this book also are 'A Pastoral,' in which we learn
to know John Todd, that typical shepherd of the Pentlands, and his dogs; the charming paper on 'The Character of Dogs,' and four literary essays beginning with
an account of his early purchases in the old book shop
in Leith Walk, and ending in 'A Humble Remonstrance,'
with a summary of his views on romance writing, and
what it really ought to be.

Somewhat of the nature too of essays or sketches is
that delightful volume, made up of different chapters in
a most ideal life, *The Silverado Squatters*, published in
1883, in which Mr Stevenson gives a brilliant description
of the very primitive existence he and his wife with Mr
Lloyd Osbourne, then a very small boy indeed, led shortly
after their marriage, in a disused miner's house—if one
can by courtesy call a *house* the three-roomed shed, into
which sunlight and air poured through the gaping boards
and the shattered windows!—on the slope of Mount
Saint Helena, where once had been the Silverado silver
mine.

Primitive in the extreme, the life must nevertheless
have been delightful; and, given congenial companionship and the perfect climate of a Californian summer,
one can imagine no more blissful experience than 'roughing it' in that sheltered cañon on the mountain side

with the ravine close below, and the most marvellous
stretch of earth, and sea, and sky, hill and plain, spread
out like an ever-changing picture before the eyes, while
to the ears there came no sound more harsh than the
shrill notes of the woodland birds.   There came also
the noise of the rattlesnake very often, Mr Stevenson
says, but they did not realise its sinister significance
until almost the end of their sojourn there, when their
attention was drawn to it, and certainly no evil befell
them.

Silverado Squatters, like *The Vailima Letters*, shows
to perfection how simple and how busy, with the most
primitive household details, the Stevensons often were
on their wanderings, and how supremely happy people,
whose tastes and habits suit each other, can be without
the artificial surroundings and luxuries of society and
civilisation that most folk consider well-nigh necessary
to their salvation.

One of the most beautiful descriptions of nature in
all Mr Stevenson's books, is that of the sea mist rising
from the Pacific, and seen from above, like a vast
white billowy ocean, by the squatters on their mountain
ledge.   Bret Harte, for whom and for whose works Mr
Stevenson had a sincere admiration, also alludes graphically to the curious scenic effects of the mist rising from
the Pacific.   Very interesting, too, are the papers on wine
and wine-growers, and the two vineyards on the mountain side ; and Scotch hearts, warm even to the Scotch
tramp who looked in at the door, and to the various
fellow-countrymen who arrived to shake hands with Mr
Stevenson because he was a Scot and like themselves,

aṇ alien from the grey skies and the clanging church bells of home.

> 'From the dim sheiling on the misty island
> Mountains divide us and a world of seas,
> Yet still our hearts are true, our hearts are Highland,'

he quotes and adds—

> 'And Highland and Lowland all our hearts are Scotch.' *

---

* Mr Stevenson was very fond of this quotation, which appeals so truly to Caledonia's sons and daughters. He found it in an old volume of *Good Words*, and never knew its source. Like many other people he quoted it incorrectly. According to information kindly supplied by Mr W. Keith Leask, the lines, which have an interesting history, stand thus in the original—

> 'From the lone sheiling on the misty island
> Mountains divide us and a waste of seas,
> Yet still the blood is strong, the heart is Highland,
> And we in dreams behold the Hebrides.'

In *Tait's Magazine* for 1849 it is given as 'Canadian Boat Song, from the Gaelic.' The author of the English version was Burns' 'Sodger Hugh,' the 12th Earl of Eglinton, who was M.P. for Ayrshire from 1784 to 1789, and was the great-grandfather of the present Earl. When in Canada the author is said to have heard a song of lament sung by evicted Hebridean crofters in Manitoba, which gave him the idea for his verses—the first four lines, and chorus, of which are—

> 'Listen to me as when we heard our father
> Sing long ago the song of other shores ;
> Listen to me, and then in chorus gather
> All your deep voices as ye pull your oars.
> *Chorus*—Fair the broad meads, these hoary woods are grand,
> But we are exiles from our fathers' land.'

Professor Mackinnon believes that the Gaelic version, known in the Highlands to this day, is founded upon the Earl of Eglinton's lines, and is not, as might be supposed, an earlier form of the poem which is known and loved by Scotch folk all the world over.

One last notice of his prose is connected with Edinburgh, and very probably with a church charity, for to help some such sale as churches patronise he wrote *The Charity Bazaar : a Dialogue*, which was given to me by its author at 17 Heriot Row one day very long ago, and which, rather frayed and yellow, is still safely pasted in my Everyday Book with the initials ' R. L. S.' in strong black writing at the end of it.

Mr Stevenson has done so much in prose that the general reader is very prone to forget those four thin volumes of verse which alone would have done much to establish his fame as an author. The first published in 1885 was *The Child's Garden of Verses*, and anything more dainty than the style and the composition of that really wonderful little book cannot be imagined, nor has there ever been written anything, in prose or in verse, more true to the thoughts and the feelings of an imaginative child.

Ballads, published in 1890 by Messrs Chatto & Windus, the firm who have published all the essays, is a collection of very interesting narrative poems. The first two, ' Rahéro, a Legend of Tahiti ' and ' The Feast of Famine, Marquesan Manners,' deal with native life in the sunny islands of the tropics, and show, with the same graphic and powerful touch as his South Sea tales do, that human life, love, hatred, and revenge are as fierce and as terrible there as in the sterner north. With the north are associated the old and curious Scotch legends, *Ticonderoga* and *Heather Ale*. The first gives in easily flowing lines a Highland slaying, the rather mean appeal of the slayer for protection to the dead man's brother and the honourable fashion in which the living Cameron elects to stand by his oath to the stranger in spite of the three times repeated complaint and curse of his dead brother. The spectre tells him that he will die at a place called Ticonderoga, but such a word is known to no man, and yet, when Pitt sends a Highland regiment, in which Captain Cameron is an officer, to America, the doomed man sees his own wraith look at him from the water, and knows, when he hears the place is Ticonderoga, he will be the first to fall in battle there.

The *Heather Ale* is a Galloway legend which tells how the last Pict on the Galloway moors prefers to see his son drowned and to die himself rather than sell his honour and betray his secret to the King.

Christmas at Sea is a sad little tale of how, when all men are glad on board the labouring ship—that stormy Christmas Day—that she has at last cleared the dangerous headland and is safely out at sea, the lad who has left the old folk to run away to be a sailor can only see the lighted home behind the coastguard's house,

> 'The pleasant room, the pleasant faces there,
> My mother's silver spectacles, my father's silver hair . . .
> . . . And oh the wicked fool I seemed in every kind of way
> To be here hauling frozen ropes on Blesséd Christmas Day . . .
> . . . They heaved a mighty breath, every soul on board but me,
> As they saw her nose again pointing handsome out to sea.
> But all that I could think of in the darkness and the cold
> Was just that I was leaving home and my folks were growing old.'

Underwoods was published by the same firm in 1887, and is most touchingly dedicated to all the many doctors of whose skill and kindness Mr Stevenson had had such frequent need. The verses in it were written at different times and in different places, and while many of them are full of the early freshness of youth some of them give as pleasantly and quaintly the riper wisdom of manhood.

Several of the verses are written to friends or relatives, some very charming lines are to his father.

Eight lines called 'The Requiem' seem the very perfection of his own idea of a last resting-place, and are almost prophetic of that lone hill-top where he lies.

Book II. of *Underwoods* is 'In Scots,' very forcible and graphic Scots too, but as to the dialect Mr Stevenson himself disarms criticism. He find his words, he says, in all localities; he spells them, he allows, sometimes with a compromise.

'I have stuck for the most part to the proper spelling,' he writes; and again—

'To some the situation is exhilarating; as for me I give one bubbling cry and sink. The compromise at which I have arrived is indefensible, and I have no thought of trying to defend it.'

And indeed he has no need of it; it is good, forcible 'Scots' after all, and the thoughts he clothes in it are as 'hame-ower' and as pithy as the words.

The Maker to Posterity, Ille Terrarum, A Blast, A Counterblast, and *The Counterblast Ironical,* are all excellent; and one can point to no prettier picture of a Scottish Sunday than *A Lowden Sabbath Morn,* which has recently been published alone in book form very nicely illustrated, while he pokes some, not undeserved, fun at our Scottish good opinion of ourselves and our religious privileges in *Embro her Kirk,* and *The Scotsman's Return from Abroad.* Surely nowhere is there Scots more musical

or lines more true to the sad experience which life brings
to us ail than these with which the book ends:

> 'It's an overcome sooth for age and youth,
>   And it brooks wi' nae denial,
> That the dearest friends are the auldest friends
>   And the young are just on trial.

> 'There's a rival bauld wi' young an' auld,
>   And it's him that has bereft me,
> For the surest friends are the auldest friends
>   And the maist o' mine hae left me.' . . .

The last volume of verses, *Songs of Travel,* has a pathos
all its own, for, like *St Ives* and *Weir of Hermiston,* the
author never saw it in print.   The verses were sent home
shortly before his death, and in the note appended to them
Mr Sidney Colvin says they were to be finally printed as
Book III. of *Underwoods,* but meantime were given to
the world in their present form in 1896.

They were written at different periods, and they show
their author in varying moods; but they incline rather to
the sadder spirit of the last two years of his life, and have
left behind them something, if not of the courage for the
fight, at least of the gaiety of living.   Two of them are
written to his wife, many of them to friends; some of them
have the lilt and the brightness of songs, others, like *If
this were Faith* and *The Woodman,* are filled with the
gravity of life and the bitterness of the whole world's
struggle for existence.

In *The Vagabond* he is still in love with the open
air life and the freedom of the tramp.   In his exile he
longs to rest at last beside those he loves; he feels the
weariness of life, he writes—

> ' I have trod the upward and the downward slope ;
> I have endured and done in days before ;
> I have longed for all, and bid farewell to hope ;
> And I have lived, and loved, and closed the door.'

After that one feels no surprise that he is waiting for the final summons, and one has only a sense of the eternal fitness of things when in the last words of the book he says—

> ' I hear the signal, Lord,—I understand
> The night at Thy command
> Comes.   I will eat and sleep, and will not question more.'

CHAPTER X

'. . . Thy genius mingles strength with grace,
. . . 'Neath thy spell the world grows fair ;
Our hearts revive, our inmost souls are stirred,
And all our English race awaits thy latest word.'
        —Sir L. MORRIS'
        Birthday Ode to the late Lord Tennyson.

BEGINNING his literary career as a writer of such quaint books of travel as *An Inland Voyage* and *Through the Cevennes with a Donkey*, such charming essays as *Roads, Ordered South, El Dorado*, and many others, Mr Stevenson was not long in entering the arena as a story-teller. His first printed stories were *A Lodging for the Night*, which appeared in *Temple Bar* in October 1877 ; *The Sire de Maletroit's Door*, in the same magazine in January 1878 ; and *Will o' the Mill*, in *Cornhill*, also in January 1878.

In *Cornhill*, in 1876 had appeared the series of essays republished as *Virginibus Puerisque*, and in 1877 and 1878 those afterwards collected under the title *Familiar Studies of Men and Books*. There also began, now and then, to be short stories from his pen in *Cornhill, Macmillan, Longmans*, Mr H. Norman's *Christmas Annual, The Court and Society Review*, and other magazines.

These, as they added originality and a certain weirdness of plot to his already recognised beauty of style, still further attracted that cultured public which had at once accepted his earlier work as that of a master of English. As already stated, it was *Will o' the Mill*, a charmingly written story of still life, with a quiet philosophy all its own, that Mr Hamerton had pronounced a masterpiece of style. *Markheim* was a graphic, but very unpleasant, story of a murder; *Olalla*, a horrible, but powerfully written, sketch of hereditary insanity, with a beautiful setting of Italian scenery to relieve the gloomy picture.

Thrawn Janet which, with most of the tales in *The Merry Men*, was written at Pitlochry, appeared in *Cornhill* in 1880. Mr Stevenson himself considered it one of his best stories, and thought it an excellent piece of dialect writing. It is weird and impressive in the extreme, and no one who has read it is likely to forget the minister of Balweary in the vale of Dull, and his terrible experiences in the matter of a housekeeper; the 'het lowin' wind' and the coppery sky of that day on which he met the black man coming down by Dull water, and knew that he had spoken with the enemy of souls himself; or the awful storm, in which Satan finally came for all that was left of Thrawn Janet. Into this story of a few pages are condensed a power of forcible expression and a weirdness of theme which have not been surpassed in any of the larger books.

The Merry Men is a story of wreck and wickedness on a desolate West Highland island where the rocks called 'the Merry Men,' as the tides boil and foam among them, make, as it were, an undercurrent of mad laughter that forms a fitting accompaniment to the hideous passions of greed and murder and the dead level of human misery that are the prevailing atmosphere of the tale. It is one of the best of the stories forming the volume, to which it gives its name, published by Messrs Chatto & Windus in 1887.

In another collection of short tales Mr Stevenson also deals with the seamy side of life, and *The New Arabian Nights* published in 1882, and which contains the reprint of such stories as *The Suicide Club, The Rajah's Diamond, The Sire de Maletroit's Door,* and *The Pavilion on the Links,* is quite as gruesome and by no means less interesting than *The Merry Men.*

The Sire de Maletroit's Door and *The Pavilion on the Links,* are most graphically written, especially the latter with its splendid description of the dreary sea and the wide and wind-swept stretch of drearier links where the curious characters play their mysterious parts. It is interesting to know that Mr Stevenson wrote *The Pavilion on the Links* while he was very ill in California. All the stories in the two volumes are favourites, and many readers give a preference to *The Suicide Club, The Rajah's Diamond,* or *Prince Florizel.*

Providence and the Guitar is also one of his best stories. *Prince Otto,* the first draft of which was written at Monterey, is the peculiar but very beautifully written story of a prince with no fancy for princedom and no talent for governing, who leaves his vain young wife and his unscrupulous prime minister in power and goes roaming among his subjects only to hear some far from complimentary opinions of himself. In the end both prince

and princess learn love and wisdom and find happiness
in spite of the revolution that drives them from their tiny
kingdom. It is a fanciful tale, the charm of which lies
less in the rather vague characters, who have the haziness
of motive and of personality of the figures in some old
play, than in the absolute perfection of style and of
description that make it a book to read and re-read with
infinite pleasure.

Mr Stevenson says, in its dedicatory preface, that he
meant to make of it a masterpiece; if he did not succeed
in doing so, as a story, he certainly gave in it a picture
of the woods so true to nature and so exquisite in style
and in expression that it will live as among his best work.

Good as this earlier writing was he had not yet found
in it his full inspiration, and it hardly appealed to so wide
a public as the fresh and delightful stories of adventure to
which he finally turned his attention. In connection with
Mr Stevenson's fiction, it is interesting to note that in his
boyhood he greatly enjoyed the stories of a novelist called
Smith, who at that time contributed to the *London
Journal*, and whose work had its influence on the boy's
future tales. Smith's novels were full of stirring adventures, and many lads of that day, besides the aspiring
novelist, were much impressed by them, and can even
now recall incidents in them read so long ago as 1858!

He had applied for work to Mr Henderson, the Scotch
editor of *Young Folks*, and to the acceptance of this
application the world owes *Treasure Island* and the
charming stories which followed it. The editor of *Young
Folks*, who offered to take a story from him, showed him
a treasure-hunting tale by Mr Peace, and asked him to

give him something on the same lines.   The result was *The Sea Cook,* which, under the altered name of *Treasure Island,* appeared in the paper in the autumn of 1881, and was not very highly paid for.   It was written under the nom-de-plume of Captain North to give the idea the author was a sailor; it was not given a very important place in the paper and it had no very marked success as a serial. It was, with very little alteration, published by Messrs Cassell & Co. in 1883, and had an instant and well-deserved success.   It is an excellent book for boys, full of stirring adventure, in the old-time fashion of fifty years ago, but it is much more; it is a book that grown-up folk, whose taste is still fresh enough to enjoy a good tale of the sea, delight in as heartily as the juniors.   It was written while the Stevenson family were staying for a time at Braemar, and Mr Thomas Stevenson gave his son valuable help in it from his own experiences at sea while on his cruises of inspection round the coasts.

The Black Arrow also appeared in *Young Folks* during 1883 as by Captain North; it is said to have been very successful as a serial, but it has not been a great favourite in book form, and is one of the least interesting of his stories.

Kidnapped came out in 1886 in the same paper and was the first to be signed as by Robert Louis Stevenson. In its serial form it was not highly paid for but it had, when Messrs Cassell & Co. published it as a book, a large and an immediate success.   It forms the first in-stalment of the delightful experiences of David Balfour, that somewhat pawky young Scot who, from the moment he leaves ' The Hawes Inn ' at Queensferry and embarks on his adventures with Alan Breck and other strange worthies in Appin and elsewhere till we finally bid him good-bye on the last page of *Catriona*, never fails at odd times and places to remind one of Mr Stevenson himself at David's age and of what he might have been and done had David Balfour's fate been his in those early days of plot and turmoil in which his part is played.

Catriona, which is a continuation of *Kidnapped*, at first appeared in *Atalanta*, and was published in book form by Messrs Cassell & Co. in 1893. In the recent edition of 1898 both volumes are brought out as *The History of David Balfour*, and are beautifully illustrated. *Catriona* is a charming book, full of life and action, and the breezy, outdoor existence, in the picturing of which its author excels. The Edinburgh of the last half of the eighteenth century, with its quaint closes, and quainter manners, is admirably portrayed, and the old lady with whom Catriona lives, and Lord Prestongrange and his daughters, are very clever pictures from a bygone day. Indeed, Miss Grant is one of the best drawn women in all Mr Stevenson's books; she has life and reality in a greater degree than most of his female characters. She is true to feminine human nature in any age, and as she makes eyes at David Balfour from under her plumed hat, and flirts with him across the narrow close, she is very woman, and alive enough to be some later day judge's daughter of modern Edinburgh, coquetting with Mr Stevenson himself, while she playfully adjusts her becoming head-gear, and lets her long feathers droop to the best advantage.

She and the two Kirsties in the unfinished *Weir of Hermiston* stand out alone among all the heroines in Mr

Stevenson's books as real breathing, living women.   They
are natural, they are possible, they have life and interest;
all the rest are more or less lay figures put in because a
heroine is necessary—the more's the pity evidently from
the author's point of view !—and drawn somewhat per-
functorily by their creator, with but a limited knowledge
of the virtues, the faults, the failings, and, above all, the
'little ways,' which go to make up the ordinary woman.

The women are undoubtedly a weakness in the
author's work.   It looks as if he had known intimately
only exceptional women,—who, possibly, had left behind
them, before he knew them well, most of a young girl's
faults and follies, and some of her attractions also,—and
had never found other women worth studying deeply, so
that the girls in his books do not read *real* enough to
interest one greatly, and it is almost a relief to take up
Treasure Island, *The Wrecker*, or *The Ebb Tide*, in which
there is very little about them.   Lady Violet Greville, in
a recent article, expresses much the same opinion.   She
says, ' The late Robert Louis Stevenson had no opinion of
women writers, he said they were incapable of grasping the
essential facts of life.   He was a great master of style, but I
doubt if he had much knowledge of feminine character '
—a dictum in which many women will agree with her.
She goes on to say that there is some truth in what he
says of women writers, because women and men regard
as essential quite different facts in life ; and she explains
it by saying that it is the difference of personality and of
point of view.   Certainly Mr Stevenson's point of view
in regard to his heroines is not a satisfying one to most
women.

Many men have drawn excellent female characters, just as a few women have given us life-like heroes. These exceptions, one imagines, must have been to some extent better able to appreciate the other sex thoroughly than most writers ; but it strikes one as odd that Mr Stevenson, who had in himself so much of gentleness and of the essentially feminine, should have so continually failed to give a living interest to his heroines. Possibly had he lived longer, and had the maturing of his powers, so evident in *Weir of Hermiston*, been accompanied by a measure of improved health, the women of his later books might all have been as powerful creations as the two Kirsties promised to be.

His heroes are all that heart can desire, manly, brave, and natural; his villains make villainy interesting; so it may be forgiven him that scarcely one of his feminine characters lives in the reader's memory.

One of the most widely known of his books is that curious story, published in 1886, called *The Strange Case of Dr Jekyll and Mr Hyde*, the popularity of which, especially in America, was immense. It deals with man's dual nature, and while Dr Jekyll embodies the good side of it, Mr Hyde, with whom he is compelled continually to exchange bodies, as well as souls, is the evil side, and commits crimes so atrocious, that the miserable doctor is well-nigh driven to despair. It is a powerful subject, powerfully treated, and contains in its small compass more moral teaching than a hundred sermons. It has, particularly in America, been used by many clergymen as the foundation of their homilies.

The Master of Ballantrae, a weird and striking tale of

the times of ' the forty-five,' is extraordinarily graphic both in its descriptions of places and of people.   The gloomy house of Durrisdeer, with its stately panelled hall, the fine grounds so carefully laid out, the thick shrubberies, the spot where the duel was fought on the hard, frozen ground by the light of the flickering candles in the tall silver candlesticks, the wave-beaten point where the smuggling luggers land goods and passengers, and finally the awful journey through the uncleared woods of America, make a fit setting, in our memories, for the splendidly drawn pictures of the three Duries, the old father, the un-appreciated Henry, the mocking master, their faithful land-steward, Mackellar, and the more shadowy person-alities of the Frenchman, the lady, and the children. The tale is one of unrelieved horror, but it is a master-piece nevertheless, and it has had a very large sale.

With his wife Mr Stevenson in *More New Arabian Nights* and *The Dynamiter* did some work of considerable interest, and with his step-son, Mr Lloyd Osbourne, he wrote that quaint tale, *The Wrong Box*.   In collaboration also with Mr Lloyd Osbourne he wrote *The Wrecker* and *The Ebb Tide*.

The Wrecker is a wild and interesting story which had a large success.   It originally appeared in *Scribner's Magazine* from August 1891 to July 1892, and was republished in book form by Messrs Cassell & Co. The scene is constantly changing in it, and the hero visits Edinburgh, stays in the students' quarter in Paris, personally conducts speculative picnics at San Francisco, distinguishes himself at the wreck on the lonely reef in mid-ocean, and finally, after appearing in England and

Fontainbleau, tells his wonderful story to a friendly trader in the south seas. There is plenty of life and of action in the tale, and there are also some delightful descriptions of the Pacific and of the wonderful glamour lagoons and palm trees throw over the spirit of the man who learns to know and to love the beautiful South Sea islands.

The Ebb Tide, originally published in Mr Jerome K. Jerome's magazine *To-day* from November 1893 to February 1894, was republished in book form by Mr W. Heinemann in 1894. Like *Treasure Island* it is a tale without a heroine, almost, indeed, without the mention of a woman except Attwater's statuesque native servant and the shadowy personalities of Herrick's mother and fiancée in London, and Captain Davis's wife and his little girl, who died before she got the doll he had so carefully bought for her, and the memory of whom is the one soft spot in his dark soul. They are merely mentioned, however, and take no actual part in the story. It is not a pleasant tale, everyone in it is more or less bad ; *more* by preference rather than less !—and for no one in it can one feel the slightest sympathy. There are villains and villains in fiction, and for some of them, for instance, Bret Harte's Jack Hamlin, or even the Master himself in *The Master of Ballantrae*, one can feel a sincere affection or at least have a grudging sort of admiration, but it is not possible to even faintly like or hesitatingly pity a cowardly Robert Herrick, whose self-pity is so strong, and who from first to last is, as his creator intended him to be, a thorough inefficient. Half-hearted in his wickedness, self-saving in his repentance, he somehow fails to

interest one ; and even his lower-class associates, the
horrible Huish and the American captain, are almost
less detestable.   Huish is quite diabolical, but he, at
least, has the courage of his iniquities.   Attwater is
not attractive either as villain or as religious enthusiast,
but he is a fairly possible character and at least a degree
less unpleasant than the American captain after his con-
version.   Captain Davis's effort to save Herrick's soul,
given in the last paragraph of the book, is disagreeably
profane in its familiarity with things sacred.   Altogether
it is not an attractive book, although it is an undoubtedly
clever one ; it has some redeeming features in the really
lovely descriptions of the island and the lagoon ; and the
appearance of the divers in full working costume remind
one of Mr Stevenson's own early experience in a diver's
dress.

Without collaboration Mr Stevenson wrote the three
pretty little tales of South Sea life reprinted, as *Island
Nights' Entertainments,* in book form about 1893.   *The
Beach of Falésa* was published in *The Illustrated London
News* from July 2nd to August 6th, 1892.   *The Bottle
Imp* appeared in *Black and White* from March 28th to
April 4th, 1891, and *The Isle of Voices* was in *The
National Observer* between 4th and 25th February of
1893.

They are charming stories, rich in local colour, and in
all of them one sees that Mr Stevenson's quick eye for the
essential in life has shown to him that among these simple
islanders are to be found just the same elements of
romance as among more highly civilised peoples, the
same motives make and influence character there as

elsewhere. So in Wiltshire and his relations with the islanders, in the curious stories of *The Bottle Imp* and *The Isle of Voices*, we are interested in a new set of people in fresh surroundings, and can in a large measure sympathise with the pleasure that the Samoans had in reading these tales of island life in their own tongue. *The Bottle Imp* was the first story ever read by the Samoans in their native language, and it raised their affection for ' Tusitala, the Teller of Stories' to positive enthusiasm.

St Ives is a bright story of adventure which Mr Stevenson had almost completed, and which Mr Quiller Couch was enabled very skilfully to finish with the assistance of the author's step-daughter, Mrs Strong, who had, besides being its amanuensis, helped Mr Stevenson with this story and been much in his confidence regarding it. It appeared first in *The Pall Mall Magazine* where it was received with favour. It is the history of a French prisoner in Edinburgh Castle during the wars of the great Napoleon. He makes, like the other prisoners, little carved ornaments for sale, and Flora, the heroine, has so touched him while buying these that he falls in love with her and presents her with a carved lion. She returns his sentiment of admiration, and after his escape she and her brother, a natural gentlemanly lad, hide Mr St Ives in the henhouse at Swanston Cottage where they live with a stern old aunt. The aunt is a well-drawn type of old-fashioned Scotchwoman, infinitely more natural and more interesting than the niece. In Edinburgh and round Mr Stevenson's own country home Swanston, the interest at first largely centres, and the writer gives a very graphic description of the home garden and the cottage and its outhouses,

'Marvellous places though handy to home.'

One imagines the tales of John Todd the shepherd must have helped much in his splendid description of the escape into England with the drovers by the solitary drove roads, at one point of which the escaping prisoner has the honour of meeting and conversing with 'The Shirra,' so well loved on Tweed side and elsewhere. After many and marvellous adventures, Mr St Ives returns a free and pardoned man to sue, not in vain, for the hand of Flora.

Last, but, if one may judge by its powerful beginning, which is, alas! all that the master-hand had left of it, certainly best of Mr Stevenson's work is *Weir of Hermiston*. In the few perfectly finished chapters there is a fulness of power and a perfection of style that promised great things. As one read the description of the fierce old judge, his gentle artistic son, the cunning dandified friend, the two Kirsties, and the four black Elliot brothers, one felt that here indeed was congenial matter; and that in the tragedy of fierce human passion about to be played out amid wild moorland surroundings, Mr Stevenson would rise to a greater perfection and a nobler success than he had yet attained to. . . . It was not to be, the busy brain stopped instantaneously, the pen that had worked so happily all the morning was laid by for ever; and the world is infinitely the poorer for the sudden catastrophe of that sad December evening which left the home at Vailima desolate.

·   ·   ·   ·   ·   ·

The beautiful *Edinburgh Edition* of Mr Stevenson's works—which his friends Mr Colvin and Mr Baxter have been seeing through the press—is almost completed ; one, or at most, two volumes only being now unpublished. It consists of an edition of 1035 copies, and includes the plays and everything of interest that he has written, and it will number twenty-seven or perhaps twenty-eight volumes. While this book has been passing through the press, volume twenty-seventh has been issued. It contains *St Ives*, and practically completes the edition ; but Mr Stevenson's widow and Mr Sidney Colvin, who are acting as his executor and his editor, have gratuitously given to the subscribers to this *Edinburgh Edition* a twenty-eighth volume, consisting of various odds and ends not hitherto made public. Of this,* 'A New Form of Intermittent Light for Lighthouses' and 'The Thermal Influence of Forests,' recall the period of his engineering and scientific training ; and the interesting facsimile reproductions of the quaint 'Moral Emblems,' written by him at Davos in 1880 and 1882, and printed with illustrations on a toy printing press by the then very youthful Mr Lloyd Osbourne, are yet another proof that even in his time of acute invalidism he was busily and cheerily employed.

* Mr Stevenson read his paper on 'A New Form of Intermittent Light for Lighthouses' before the Royal Scottish Society of Arts in 1871, and received a silver medal for it. Two years later his paper on 'The Thermal Influence of Forests' was contributed to the Royal Society of Edinburgh.

CHAPTER XI.

HIS LIFE IN SAMOA

'Sometimes I am hopeful as the spring,
And up my fluttering heart is borne aloft
As high and gladsome as the lark at sunrise,
And then as though some fowler's shaft had pierced it
It comes plumb down in such a dead, dead fall.'
—FROM *Philip Van Artevelde.*

MR THOMAS STEVENSON died early in May 1887, having lived long enough to see his son's fame as an author firmly established. Not very long afterwards Mrs Thomas Stevenson joined her son and his wife and with them went to America, and on that yachting tour among the South Sea islands, which finally resulted in the purchase, by Robert Louis, of the little property on the slope of the Vaea mountain, above the town of Apia, in Samoa, which he called by the musical name of Vailima, and where, in 1890, he finally made his home.

His mother returned to Scotland for some months in 1889, arriving in the June of that year and remaining till the October of 1890, when she joined her son and his wife in their Samoan home. In 1893 she again visited Edinburgh to see her relatives there, and to arrange for the breaking up of the home at 17 Heriot Row, the sale of the house and of such things as she

did not care to keep or to take with her to that new
home which she also intended to make her headquarters.
She remained on this occasion almost a year, and left
for London, en route for Samoa, on the 5th of March
1894, promising her relatives and her friends, who so
greatly grudged her to her son and his household, that
she would pay a visit to Scotland once every five years.

Alas! in less than one year her son had followed his
father into the Life Eternal, and she was left that most
desolate of all mourners 'a widow and childless.' She
remained for a little time with her daughter-in-law and
the sorrow-stricken Vailima household, and on 1st June
1895 she arrived in Edinburgh to make her home with
her sister, Miss Balfour, as that sister so touchingly
expresses it, 'a desolate woman.'

Much was left to her in the love of relatives and
friends, and in her own bright spirit, which, while it
recalled the happiness of the past, never repined at the
emptiness of the present; but so much of her heart lay
buried in her two graves that one dared not murmur,
nay, one could hardly fail to rejoice for her, when, early
in May 1897, she too passed into her rest, most deeply
mourned by all who had so dearly loved her, and not
least by the little children who had held so warm a
place in her affections, and whose spontaneous offering
of flowers so touched and comforted the sad hearts of
her sorrowing relatives.

In his mother's letters to her sister and to other
members of her family—so often kindly read to friends
—one had almost as graphic an account of Mr Stevenson's Samoan home as in the delightful volume of *Vailima*

Letters itself. Gifted also with a fluent pen and a keen interest in the details which make up life, the mother like the son wrote charmingly; and one laughed, as one does in *The Vailima Letters*, over such misfortunes as the raid of the little pigs among the young corn; the more or less serious peccadilloes of the childlike Samoan servants; and that crowning catastrophe, so comically described by Mr Stevenson, when the carpenter's horse put its foot into a nest of fourteen eggs, and 'made an omelette of all their hopes'!

Nothing could have been more delightful or more amusing than that unconventional sunny life to people who like the Stevensons were perfectly happy among themselves, and, in spite of the often serious anxieties and worries incident on their settling in the new home, absolutely contented with their surroundings. The out-of-door existence, the free, untrammelled life, was dear to all of them, and especially good for Mr Stevenson; and far from the hurry and bustle of towns they found, under the unclouded blue of the Samoan sky, the rest and the peace their souls had longed for.

The climate worked wonders for Mr Stevenson, and it seemed hardly possible to believe that the pale shadow of the Bournemouth days was the active owner of Vailima, who himself worked untiringly in clearing the scrub, and making the rank, tropical bush give place to the ordered beauties of civilisation. Not only he but his wife cheerfully took a turn in weeding, and, hot, tired, and with skins blistered by the poisonous plants with which war had to be waged by hand, they themselves did as much as, if not more than, their Samoan assistants to eradicate the noxious growths and make the precious blades of grass spring up in their place. Yet glad as they were to welcome the grass, Mr Stevenson, as he pulled the weeds up, hated to cause their death, and felt that they were victims in the great war of life against life of which the world is full.

Existence at Vailima was simple and patriarchal in the extreme. The Samoans, who found in its owner so kind and so staunch a friend, had the warm hearts, the natural good qualities of children, but they had some of the vices of untrained children also, and petty thefts and tiresome acts of disobedience, gave their master and mistress abundant trouble, and often necessitated a species of impromptu court of justice, in which Mr Stevenson distributed reproofs and meted out punishments to the offenders in the midst of a full gathering of the domestic staff, both indoor and out, who all looked up to him much as one fancies the desert herdsmen did to Abraham, or as in later days the Highland clansmen feared and yet worshipped their chief, whose word was law.

His wife's ready wit on at least one occasion showed itself by utilising the native superstition to bring home the enormity of the offence to the possible stealer of a young pig. The fear of an 'Aitu,' or wicked woman-spirit of the woods, and the general dread of devils, has far more effect on the Samoan conscience than more civilised methods of warning and reproof. So when Mrs Stevenson, by a clever imitation of native conjuring, made Lafaele believe that 'her devil,' or divining spirit, would tell her where the missing pig was, it is probable that Lafaele, even if innocent himself, shared the feast with his friends with trembling.

The master and mistress had the kindest interest in all their native servants, and it is a quaint thing to read of the great writer, for whose books publishers and public impatiently waited, not only giving Mr Strong's little boy, Austin, history lessons, but spending hours over teaching Henry, the Samoan chief, who was his native overseer. Very strange, too, it is to realise that he carried his interest in missions and missionaries to so practical a point as for a time at least to teach Sunday school himself. His stepson, Mr Lloyd Osbourne, shared to the full his interest in these things, and both of them must have been very comforting to the missionaries in Samoa, one of whom especially, Mr Clark, was so valued a friend of the whole Vailima household. The Roman Catholic priests, many of whom are doing devoted work in the islands, were also welcome visitors at Vailima.

Never bound by creeds or forms, Mr Stevenson had a thoroughly practical religion, calculated to do infinitely more good in the world than all the theological disputes and hair splittings that ever were penned in ponderous volumes or thundered solemnly from orthodox pulpits.

Of his political work in Samoa, his earnestness for the good government of its people, his anxiety that they should have a just control and a due freedom, it is unnecessary to speak fully here, as his letters in the home press at the time and the volume *Footnotes to History* brought the knowledge of his views and actions within reach of all. Nothing could have been more unselfish than the attitude of the writer, to whom politics were abhorrent, who, nevertheless, from sheer humanity entered, at some personal risk, into the petty struggle with excellent results for the Samoans. And certainly nothing more courageous can be imagined than the man, whose tender heart winced at the sight of suffering and bloodshed, going down into the hospitals during the brief war, and himself helping to tend and comfort the wounded and the dying. In his interest in native affairs he had, as in all else that made up life for him, the thorough sympathy of his wife, and also of the other members of his most united household.

It was a very happy party in spite of some misfortunes and anxieties, occasional visits of the influenza, and the dread of ruin from rain or hurricane; and after their first difficulties as to house-building were over, it was to a very spacious and pleasant house that they welcomed the elder Mrs Stevenson when she returned to Samoa in 1893. The scrub still, however, required much clearing, and we find in *The Vailima Letters* Mr Stevenson dividing his day into so many hours of literary work and so many hours of weeding!

The day began early, and Mr Stevenson, after the first breakfast, did his literary work, until the sound of a conch summoned the family to a lunch, or second breakfast, about eleven o'clock. After this there was rest and music till four, and then outdoor work or play, lawn-tennis being a very favourite pastime, and in the evening they had more music, and a game at cards. It was a simple, natural life, and one that made far more for health, mental and physical, to those whose constitutions suited the climate, than the bustle and the clamour of cities. Visitors, too, often came up the hill to Vailima, sometimes the residents in Apia, sometimes home friends or distinguished strangers, who were glad to visit the much-loved author in his distant retreat, and to all was given the same cordial welcome, to all there remains the memory of delightful hours in the company of those who knew so well how to make time pass bewitchingly.

The household by this time consisted of Mr Stevenson, his wife, his mother, Mr Lloyd Osbourne, his sister, Mrs Strong, who acted as her stepfather's amanuensis, her little boy, Austin, who went to school in California in 1892, and Mr Graham Balfour, a cousin of Mr Stevenson's.

Until he left for school, Mr Stevenson gave Austin his lessons, and, as his uncle Lloyd had done, the boy considered the teacher only a larger playfellow.

A very pretty picture of the home life is given in a note-book of Mrs Thomas Stevenson's, in which she describes a birthday feast in her honour, at which little Austin Strong recited some verses made for the occasion by her son. Very amusing the verses are, and in them the small scholar repeats with pride what strides in knowledge he had made under the able tuition of his step-grandfather. It is not a little comic to think that Mr Stevenson had at this time a well-grown step-grandchild, and had, indeed, held the honourable and venerable position of a step-grandparent shortly after he was thirty.

Very amusing features of the letters that Mrs Thomas Stevenson sent home were the funny illustrations of daily life enclosed in them, and which were drawn by a clever pencil in the household.   Like the old plays in the Leith Walk shop the youthful Louis once so frequently visited, they were *A Penny Plain and Twopence Coloured.*   Sometimes they were mere outlines of domestic processions, sometimes they were gay with paint in shades of brown and green and blue. In them all the members of the family were represented, and now and then there appeared the dusky semblance of a Samoan domestic Faauma, 'the bronze candlestick,' or Lafaele, the amiable and the willing. As one recalls them one sees again a verandah, with long chairs and lazy loungers, Mr Stevenson pretending to play his flageolet, but too comfortable actually to begin ; the rest in attitudes more or less suggestive of that warmth and satisfaction which we in colder climes can only dream of ; or in another a few bold strokes pictured the ladies of the family on household cares intent, domestic service of the humblest, cooking, dusting, bed-making, and all the trivial daily doings that were so mirthfully treated both by pen and pencil.

Mr Stevenson and his wife took a keen interest in their garden, which stood so high above sea-level, that they could have the pleasure of trying to grow in it some British flowers, fruits, and vegetables, as well as those native to the tropics. This endeavour to naturalise the products of the old home in the new one was a great pleasure to Mrs Stevenson, and one fully shared by her husband, who was so often, in spite of his delight in the soft airs, the blue skies, heart-sick for the cold grey ones of the old country, and who was reminded on a fresh wet morning after a storm, of the West Highlands, near Callander, and

' The smell of bog - myrtle and peat,'

by the rain dashing on the roof, and trickling down the window panes, of far-off misty Scotland, where

' On the moors the whaups are calling.'

The Samoan days were very full of work, and much was

done, and still more was planned in them by Mr Stevenson's busy brain and untiring activity.   Here was written *Catriona, The Master of Ballantrae,* a part of those annals of the Stevenson family which he hoped to give to the public, *The Beach of Falésa, The Bottle Imp,* and *The Isle of Voices*; and with Mr Lloyd Osbourne was completed *The Ebb Tide* and *The Wrecker,* the ideas for which had occurred to them when at sea.

Father Damien, An Open Letter, had been already written, but here was composed *A Footnote to History,* and both show to perfection their writer's interest in suffering humanity.   Here, saddest of all, were planned many works never to be accomplished—among them that powerful fragment *Weir of Hermiston* and *St Ives*—the latter finished all but the last portion, which Mrs Strong, who had helped much with this story, could supply to Mr Quiller Couch, so that he was enabled to complete it.   Mr Stevenson, like his father, found his relaxation in a change of work, so to this period also belong the fugitive verses collected under the title, *Songs of Travel,* published after his death.

In spite of the apparent improvement in his health, Mr Stevenson had had, especially when for a short time at Sydney and Honolulu, serious returns of illness, and after one attack of influenza, the old foe hemorrhage briefly reappeared.   Not yet, however, would he own himself beaten, and in spite of some anxiety on the part of his doctors, he assured his friends he was very well. His friends' fears were not so easily silenced.   In the last year of his life his bright mood varied, and his letters often caused grave anxiety to those at home.   He

had times of despondency and of undue distress as to his
monetary future and his literary success, which were
scarcely justified by the facts.   Although always gentle
and gay with his own family circle, the little strain of
worry showed itself repeatedly in his correspondence with
his friends and caused them a keen foreboding of evil, so
unlike was it to the old, sunny, cheery spirit with which
he had fought bad health, and gained for himself so high
a place in the world of letters and so warm a niche in the
heart of his public.

CHAPTER XII

HIS DEATH

'Gone to thy rest—no doubt, no fear, no strife;
Men whispering call it death—God calls it life.'
ROBERT RICHARDSON.

As the months of 1894 slipped away, the unusual despondency and worry, noticeable so especially in Mr
Stevenson's correspondence, increased, while it seemed
that his literary work, which had hitherto been his
greatest pleasure, had now become a strain and a
weariness to him.

By fits and starts the joy of working still visited him
it is true. *Weir of Hermiston* he felt to be his very
best—*St Ives* now and then went gaily. But the
dark moods were only dormant not dead, and anxiety
for the future of his family, and a longing to be
able to cease working for daily bread, grew upon him
greatly.

That, for a time after the settlement in Samoa,
monetary anxieties may have been somewhat pressing,
is not only possible, but probable. No moving of 'the
household gods,' however small, or for however short a
distance, can be managed without considerable cost and

141

trouble, and the expense invariably exceeds the estimate made, for unforeseen outlays and difficulties crop up that entail added expenditure with its consequent anxiety.

If this is so in ordinary cases, how much more would it be so when the pulling up of stakes meant a move to the antipodes and the change of home included the purchase of uncleared land in Samoa, the building of a house and the laying out of an estate, which its owner felt certain could not repay the money spent upon it for at least five or six years.

All great changes and large undertakings are fraught with difficulty, and the Vailima venture was no exception to the rule. The Samoan home meant much pleasure to its owner, but it entailed keen anxiety also.

Nevertheless the mental worry of those later months was by no means justified by the facts. Mr Stevenson's literary work had long been paid according to its merits, so that each book brought him in a satisfactory sum ; while the future of the *Edinburgh Edition* of his works gave cause for sincere satisfaction to the friends who were seeing it through the press, and whose letters gave assurance of its success. The cloud was therefore due to internal, not to external causes, and in the state of Mr Stevenson's health was, alas ! to be found the explanation of this sad change from the gay bravery with which he had hitherto faced the world. Suspected by his doctors, feared by his friends, but unknown to himself, for at this time he constantly wrote of his improved health, a new development in his illness was nearing its fatal crisis, and these symptoms of mental distress and irritation were only the foreshadowing of the end.

In these last days his life had many pleasures ; he was enjoying the Samoan climate and the free unconventional existence to the full ; he was surrounded by all his loved home circle ; and in the October of 1894, two months before his death, the Samoan chiefs, to whom in their imprisonment he had proved his friendship, gave him a tribute of their love and gratitude which was peculiarly pleasing and valuable to him.   An account of this and of the very beautiful speech he made in return appeared in the home papers at the time, and are to be found in an appendix to *The Vailima Letters.*   The chiefs, who knew how much store he set by road-making as a civilising element in Samoa, as elsewhere, themselves went to him and offered their services to make a road to join his property to the main highway.   They, as well as their young men, worked at it with picks and spades, and when it was finished they presented it to their beloved 'Tusitala' as an abiding remembrance of their grateful regard.   It was a noble tribute to a noble nature, and one the value of which can only be fully appreciated by those who realise what the personal manual labour meant to these proud island chiefs so wholly unaccustomed to exertion of any kind, and so imbued with the idea that all labour was derogatory to their dignity. Their loving service touched Mr Stevenson and all his family very deeply, and this bright memory gladdened the last weeks of his life, and must be a very pleasant one to recall for those of the Vailima household who still survive him.

At the celebration of his birthday on 13th November he had received also a tribute of kindly appreciation from the European and American residents in Apia. On the occasion of a ' Thanksgiving ' feast in that same November, he made a speech, in which he said he had always liked *that* day, for he felt that he had had so much for which to be thankful. He especially mentioned the pleasure he had in his mother being with him, and said that to America— where he had married his wife—he owed the chief blessing of his life.

In spite of his assurances that he was very well, he was exceedingly thin and wasted in those days, and later Samoan photographs show a melancholy change in him. On the morning of the 3rd December, however, he felt particularly well and wrote for several hours. It is very pleasant to know, from *A Letter to Mr Stevenson's Friencs,* sent to the *Times* after his stepfather's death by Mr Lloyd Osbourne as an acknowledgment of the vast amount of sympathy expressed, and so impossible to be otherwise answered, that he had enjoyed his work on *Weir of Hermiston,* and felt all the buoyancy of successful effort on that last morning of his life.

Letters for the mail were due to be written in the afternoon, and he spent his time penning long and kindly greetings to absent friends.

' At sunset,' Mr Osbourne says, ' he came downstairs, rallied his wife about the forebodings she could not shake off ; talked of a lecturing tour in America he was eager to make, " as he was so well," and played a game of cards with her to drive away her melancholy.'

By-and-bye he said that he was hungry, and proposed a little feast, for which he produced a bottle of old Burgundy, and went to help her to prepare a salad, talking gaily all the while. As they were on the verandah, he suddenly cried out, ' What is that ? ' put his hands to his head, and asked, ' Do I look strange ? ' In a moment he had fallen down beside her.

His wife called for help, and she and his body-servant Sosima carried him into the great hall, where he had known so much happiness, and placed him in the old arm-chair which had been his grandfather's. Medical aid was quickly obtained, but he had already lost consciousness, and, in spite of every effort, he never regained it. His mother's letters written after his death touchingly describe how, although called at once, she yet reached the hall too late to find him conscious, as by that time he was leaning back in his chair breathing heavily. The family, with an agony of grief, quickly realised that there was no hope.

A little bed was brought, and he was placed on it in the middle of the hall, and there, with those he loved close about him, and his faithful Samoan servants seated round him on the floor, he quietly passed away. The deep breaths came at ever longer intervals, the sleep of unconsciousness was never broken, and as his loved and valued friend, the Reverend Mr Clark, prayed beside him, his spirit took its flight into eternity. He died as he had wished, quickly and well-nigh painlessly. He had known so much of lingering illness, he dreaded *that* greatly, but of death he had no fear, and peacefully and suddenly he passed into the Unseen.

His death took place at a little past eight o'clock on the evening of the 3rd December at the early age of forty-four.

When the news was cabled to England, it was received by many people with grave doubts. His relatives and friends dreaded its truth, but could not at first believe it. Many exaggerated newspaper reports, copied especially from the more sensational American press, had from time to time caused needless distress and anxiety to those who loved him, so that it was possible to allow oneself the shadow of a hope, particularly as his uncle, Dr George W. Balfour, who had at first received the news somewhat vaguely worded, doubted it also, and wrote to the *Scotsman* expressing his unbelief.

Too soon, unfortunately, all such hopes were proved false, and eager eyes scanning the morning papers on the 23d December 1894 read this sad corroboration of the news that had been posted in London on the 17th of the same month.

'SAN FRANCISCO (no date).
          BALFOUR, 17 Walker Street, Edinburgh.
LOUIS died suddenly third.   Tell friends.
                              STEVENSON.'

The telegram was from his mother in answer to one from his uncle asking for true particulars as to the earlier report, and on its receipt and publication relatives and friends knew that hope was dead, and there remained only a sad waiting for further particulars.   These by-and-bye came in letters from his mother to her relatives and friends in Scotland, in letters to his literary friends and in that 'Letter' to the *Times* from his friend and stepson Mr Lloyd Osbourne to the vast mass of acquaintances and readers who all claimed him as a loved personal friend.

From all these sources the manner of his death, and the touching final tragedy of his pathetic funeral became known to the world of English-speaking people everywhere, who each and all mourned individually for the loved and lost author as one near and dear in their personal regard.

He had always expressed a wish to be buried on the Vaea mountain which rises immediately behind Vailima, and the summit of which commands a wide prospect of land and sea and sky. In the spring of 1894, he had suggested the making of a road, and the planting of the spot which he had chosen for his resting-place, but, as the idea was painful to his family, nothing was done in the matter. As soon as he had passed away, those whom he loved hastened to give effect to his wishes, and Mr Lloyd Osbourne planned and courageously carried out in an incredibly short time the forming of a road which made it possible to carry him to the summit of Vaea, and lay him on the spot that he had chosen. Forty Samoans with knives and axes cut a path up the mountain side, and Mr Lloyd Osbourne, with a few specially chosen dependents, dug the grave in which he was to lie.

Meantime, his body covered with the Union Jack rested in the Samoan home that he had loved so well, surrounded by the furniture of the old Scotch home around which his childish feet had played, and on which his father, and possibly his father's fathers, had daily looked, for his mother had taken with her to Vailima all that had most of memory and of family tradition from the house in Heriot Row.

His family lingered in the dear presence, the heart-broken Samoans knelt and kissed his hands, and at the request of his favourite servant, Sosima, who was a Romanist, the solemn and touching prayers of the Church of Rome were, with a certain fitness, repeated over the man who had been the champion of Father Damien, and among whose friends were numbered the earnest and faithful Roman Catholic missionary priests of the South Sea Islands.

On his coffin was laid the 'Red Ensign' that had floated from his mast on many a cruise, and he was carried up the steep path by those who loved him. Europeans as well as Samoans toiled up that difficult ascent to place him with reverent hands in that grave which was so fitting a resting-place for the man who had loved, above all things, the freedom of the open air, the glory of the sea and the sky, the sighing of God's winds among the trees, and the silent companionship of the stars.

.   .   .   .   .   .

Life for those who remained in the Samoan home became an impossible thing without him, and so Mrs Stevenson, with her son and daughter, by-and-bye left Vailima, and the home of so much happiness is now falling into ruin, the cleared ground lapsing back to the bush. And perhaps it is best so; without him Vailima is like a body without a soul; and he who so dearly loved nature would hardly have regretted that the place he loved should return to the mother heart of the earth and become once more a solitude—a green place of birds and trees.

CHAPTER XIII

HIS LIFE-WORK

'Art's life, and when we live we suffer and toil.'
—Mrs BARRETT BROWNING.

' A healthful hunger for the great idea,
The beauty and the blessedness of life.'
—JEAN INGELOW.

IT is perhaps impossible for those who knew Mr Stevenson and came under the influence of the rare attraction
of his charming personality, to assign to him and to his
work a suitable place in the world of letters.   Probably it
is still too early for anyone to say what rank will in the
future be held by the man who in his life-time assuredly
stood among the masters of his craft.   Fame, while he lived,
was his, and, better than fame, such love as is seldom
given by the public to the writer whose books delight it.

Deservedly popular as the books are, the man was still
more popular ; and the personality that to his friends was
so unique and so delightful, made friends of his readers
also.   He was so frank, so human, in his relations with
his public.

His dedications not only gave pleasure to the members
of his family, or to the many friends to whom he wrote
them, they, as it were, took his readers into his confidence also, and let them share in the warmth of his

heart.   His prefaces are delightfully autobiographical,
and are valuable in proportion to the glimpses they give
of one of the most amiable and most widely sympathetic
natures imaginable.

His methods of work were singularly conscientious ;
even in the days when, as a truant lad, he carried in
his pocket one book to read, and another to write in,
he was slowly perfecting that style which was to give
to his literary work a distinction all its own.   He spared
himself no trouble in ensuring the accuracy of all that
he wrote.

It may be interesting to recall in this connection the
letters written by two of his readers to the *Scotsman*
expressing some doubt as to there having been shops
in Princes Street at the date of his story *St Ives*—Mr
Stevenson mentions shops in *St Ives*.   In reply to
the letters of enquiry, his uncle, Dr G. W. Balfour,
wrote to the *Scotsman* on 26th November 1897 :—

'Sir,—It may interest your correspondents " J. W. G."
and " J. C. P." to know that Louis Stevenson always
took care to verify his statements before making them,
and that his correspondent, to whom he applied for
information as to the existence of shops in Princes
Street at the early date referred to, took the only legitimate means open to him of ascertaining this by consulting the directories of the date.'

And, as a matter of fact, it was conclusively proved
that Mr Stevenson was correct, by the name and number
of at least one well-known shop, of that date, being
given by another correspondent in the paper very shortly
afterwards.

No minute observation was too trying for Mr Stevenson, no careful research too tedious for him; no historical
fact apparently too insignificant or obscure for him to
verify. He was never weary of reading books dealing with
the periods in which the action of his stories takes place.

Costume, dialect, scenery, were all thoroughly studied,
and when himself distant from the scenes of his tales,
he is to be found constantly writing from Vailima to
friends in London or in Edinburgh for the books and
the information he required. In the period between
1745 and 1816, in which the plots of *Kidnapped*, *Catriona*, *The Master of Ballantrae*, *Weir of Hermiston*,
and *St Ives* are laid, he is especially at home, and old
record rolls, books on manners and on costume, are all
laboriously studied to give to his stories that accuracy
and truth to life which he considered to be absolutely
necessary. To such good effect did he study volumes
of old Parliament House trials, that the dress of Alan
Breck, in *Kidnapped*, is literally transcribed from that of
a prisoner of Alan's period, whose trial he had perused.

Nor did his conscientiousness stop here; he wrote
and re-wrote everything, sometimes as often as five times,
and no page ever left his hands which had not been elabo-
rately pruned and polished. No wonder, therefore, that
his work was welcome to his publishers, and that he was
never among the complaining authors who think themselves underpaid and unappreciated by the firms with
whom they deal.

He gave of his best, good honest hard work, and he
received in return not only money but regard and consideration; and his own verdict was that it was difficult

to choose among his publishers which should have a new book, for all of them were so good to him. A pleasant state of matters that goes far to prove that, where work is conscientious and author and publisher honourable and sensible, there need be little or no friction between them. In this, as in the care which he bestowed on his work, the long and earnest apprenticeship he served to the profession of letters, he sets an example to his fellow-authors quite as impressive as that which he showed to his fellow-men in the patience with which he bore his heavy burden of bad health, and the courage with which he rose above his sufferings and looked the world in the face smiling.

In an age when a realism so strong as to be unpleasant has tinged too much of latter-day fiction Mr Stevenson stood altogether apart from the school of the realists.   His nature, fresh and boyish to the end, troubled itself not at all with social questions, so he dipped his pen into the wells of old romance and painted for us characters so alive with strength and with humour that they live with us as friends and comrades when the creations of the problem novelists have died out of our memories with the problems they propound and worry over.

His books are bright, breezy, cheerful, rich in idealism, full of chivalry, and they have in them a glamour of genius, a power of imagination, and a spirit of purity, which makes them peculiarly valuable in an age when these things are too often conspicuous by their absence from the novel of the day.

His essays are full of a quaint, delightful humour, his verses have a dainty charm, and in his tales he has given

us a little picture gallery of characters and landscapes
which have a fascination all their own.   Like Sir Walter
Scott he had to contend with the disadvantages of a
delicate childhood which interfered with settled work ;
and yet, in both cases, one is tempted to think that that
enforced early leisure was of far more ultimate benefit to
the life-work than years of dutiful attendance at school
and college.   Like Sir Walter Scott, also, he has drawn
much of his inspiration from ' Caledonia, stern and wild ' ;
and none of her literary sons, save Burns and ' The
Wizard of the North' himself, has Caledonia loved so
well or mourned so deeply.

Cosmopolite in culture, in breadth of view, in openness
of mind, Mr Stevenson was yet before all things a Scotsman, and one to whom Scotland and his native Edinburgh
were peculiarly dear.   Condemned by his delicate and
uncertain health to make his dwelling-place far from the
grey skies and the biting east winds of his boyhood's
home, these grey Scotch skies, these bitter winds, still
haunt him and appear in his books with the strange
charm they have for the sons and daughters of the north
who, even while they revile them, love them, and in far
lands long for them with a heart-hunger that no cloudless
sky, no gentle zephyr, no unshadowed sunshine of the
alien shore can appease.*

* It is on record that Mr Stevenson, who always talked to a com-
patriot when he could, was, à propos of his home in Samoa, told by a
sailor with whom he was having a chat, that he ' would rather gang
hame an' be hanged in auld Scotland than come an' live in this ———
hole.'   No doubt, Mr Stevenson appreciated the sturdy mariner's
patriotism, although it was expressed in language more forcible than
polite !

In all his wanderings his heart turned fondly to the
old home, to the noble profession of his fathers, and on
smiling seas and amid sunny islands he never forgot the
bleak coasts of Scotland, that his ancestors' hands had
lighted from headland to headland, and his heart

'In dreams (beheld) the Hebrides.'

A Scot of whom Edinburgh and Scotland are justly
proud, he was a man whose life and faith did credit to
the stern religion and the old traditions of his covenanting
forefathers, and although, like so many men and women
of earnest minds and broad culture in the present day,
he early left behind him much of the narrowness of
churches and of creeds, he held closely to 'the one
thing needful,' a humble and a trusting belief in God
that filled all his soul with strength and patience, and
gave to him that marvellous sympathy with humanity
which made him a power among men, whether they
were the learned and the cultured, or simple children
of nature like the Samoans, who so truly understood
and loved him.

The books undoubtedly are great, but the man is
greater; and it is not only as a writer of no small renown
that he will be revered and remembered but as a man
among men whose patience and courage gave to his too
short life a pathos and a value. Among his friends he
was beloved in a manner quite unique, he had a peculiar
place of his own in their regard. By the younger school
of writers, whose work he so fully and so generously
appreciated, he was regarded as a master; and one of
the pleasures to be enjoyed on the publication of that

Life, which Mr Sidney Colvin presently has in preparation, will be to learn more about his agreeable relations with his literary juniors.

Of his sacred home life no outsider can speak ; but it is the truest test of perfect manhood when the man who is not unknown in the great world shows himself at his best in the smaller world of home, and has a brighter and a sweeter side of his nature to display to wife and mother and close fireside circle than he has to his admiring public. Mr Stevenson never despised the trivial things of life, and the everyday courtesies, the little unselfishnesses—which are often so much more difficult to practise than the great virtues—were never forgotten all through the years in which so much of pain and of weariness might have made occasional repining, occasional forgetfulness of others, almost pardonable.

Eager in his own work, untiring in his literary activity, he was equally eager to toil in the great vineyard, to do something for God and for man, to make his faith active and not passive. This was his attitude through life ; he would always have 'tholed his paiks' that the poor might 'enjoy their play,' the imprisoned go free ; and the position which he took up in regard to Samoan troubles was a practical proof that he was, as he called himself, 'a ready soldier,' willing to spend and be spent for others. Of one whose position was that of 'the ready soldier,' no more fitting concluding words can be penned than those in his mother's note-book, which were written to her by the wife of the Rev. Mr Clark, his Samoan friend, in November 1895 :—

. . . 'So few knew your dear son's best side—his

Christian character. Of course, men don't write often on that subject, and to many he was the author, and they only knew him as such. To me his lovely character was one of the wonderful things, so full of love and the desire to do good. I love to think of him.' . . .

That the man and his work are appreciated is amply proved by the monument already erected to his memory in San Francisco by the zeal of the American Committee, and by the enthusiastic meeting in his own Edinburgh, presided over by Lord Rosebery, in the autumn of 1896, at which Mr J. M. Barrie made an interesting and an appreciative speech ; and by the equally enthusiastic gathering in Dundee in the spring of 1897.

At these meetings it was proposed to receive subscriptions, and to erect a Stevenson memorial in some form to be afterwards decided on. The suggestion was largely responded to, but it is probable the response would have been even more cordial had it been determined that the memorial should take a practical rather than an ornamental form. Monuments are cold things whereby to perpetuate love and admiration ; an 'arbour of Corinthian columns,' which one paper recently suggested, would have appealed to Mr Stevenson himself only as an atrocity in stone. His sole sympathy with stone was when it served the noble purpose to which his father had put it, and, as lighthouse or harbour, contributed to the service of man. If the memorial might have been too costly in the form of a small shore-light, a lifeboat seemed a thing that would have been dear to his own heart. And as, in years to come, men read of rescues by the *Robert Louis Stevenson*, on some wreck-strewn, rock-bound corner of our coasts, the memory of the man who loved the sea, and of the race who toiled to save life in its storms, would have been handed down to future generations in a fitting fashion.

The memorial is to take the form of a mural monument with a medallion portrait of his head in high relief. It is to be placed in the Moray Aisle of St Giles' Cathedral, Edinburgh, which it is thought might be a suitable ' Poets' Corner ' for Scotland. If there is sufficient money, and if the necessary permission is obtained, a stone seat may also be erected on the Calton Hill at the point from which Mr Stevenson so greatly admired the view. The medallion is to be entrusted to Mr A. Saint Gaudens, an American sculptor of repute, who studied in France, and who had the great advantage of personally knowing Mr Stevenson in America in 1887 and 1888, and at that time getting him to sit for a medallion, which is considered by his widow and family to be the best likeness of him that they have seen. It is satisfactory that at last someone has been found who can do justice to the quaint, mobile face, and give to the memorial some of the living charm of the man. It is also pleasant to know that Mrs Stevenson and her family have expressed themselves perfectly satisfied with the choice of a sculptor.

The San Francisco monument is in the form of ' a sixteenth century ship, of thirty guns, careening to the west, with golden sails full spread, and with a figure of Pallas, looking towards the setting sun, in its prow.' The ship is about five feet high, and behind it, on a simple granite plinth, is engraved the famous passage from his Christmas sermon :—' To be honest, to be kind ; to earn a little, to spend a little less; to keep a few friends, and these without capitulations.'

On one surface of the plinth is a spigot and a cup, and underneath a drip-stone, where thirsty dogs can drink. The drinking place is assuredly a part of the monument that would have commended itself to the man who loved his canine friends and all other animals so truly.

Even if a monument has about it something of the commonplace, it is well that the memory of the man and of his work should be perpetuated; but of all memorials of him, the Samoan 'Road of Gratitude' or 'Road of Loving Hearts,' is likely to be for ever remembered as the most suitable and the most perfect.